Strange Stories from

of Leisures

Songling Pu

Alpha Editions

This edition published in 2024

ISBN : 9789362997401

Design and Setting By
Alpha Editions
www.alphaedis.com
Email - info@alphaedis.com

As per information held with us this book is in Public Domain.
This book is a reproduction of an important historical work. Alpha Editions uses the best technology to reproduce historical work in the same manner it was first published to preserve its original nature. Any marks or number seen are left intentionally to preserve its true form.

Contents

PREFACE .... - 1 -

THE GHOST IN LOVE .... - 4 -

THE FRESCO .... - 8 -

THE DWARF HUNTERS .... - 11 -

THE CORPSE THE BLOOD-DRINKER .... - 13 -

LOVE REWARDED .... - 16 -

THE WOMAN IN GREEN .... - 19 -

THE FAULT AND ITS CONSEQUENCES .... - 21 -

DECEIVING SHADOWS .... - 23 -

PEACEFUL-LIGHT .... - 26 -

HONG THE CURRIER .... - 29 -

AUTUMN-MOON .... - 33 -

THE PRINCESS NELUMBO .... - 36 -

THE TWO BROTHERS .... - 38 -

THE MARBLE ARCH .... - 41 -

THE DUTIFUL SON .... - 47 -

THROUGH MANY LIVES	- 49 -
THE RIVER OF SORROWS	- 51 -
THE MYSTERIOUS ISLAND	- 54 -
THE SPIRIT OF THE RIVER	- 56 -
THE-DEVILS-OF-THE-OCEAN	- 58 -
UNKNOWN DEVILS	- 61 -
CHILDLESS	- 63 -
THE PATCH OF LAMB'S SKIN	- 66 -
LOVE'S-SLAVE	-68 -
THE LAUGHING GHOST	- 71 -

PREFACE

The first European students who undertook to give the Western world an idea of Chinese literature were misled by the outward and profound respect affected by the Chinese towards their ancient classics. They have worked from generation to generation in order to translate more and more accurately the thirteen classics, Confucius, Mengtsz, and the others. They did not notice that, once out of school, the Chinese did not pay more attention to their classics than we do to ours: if you see a book in their hands, it will never be the "Great Study" or the "Analects," but much more likely a novel like the "History of the Three Kingdoms," or a selection of ghost-stories. These works that everybody, young or old, reads and reads again, have on the Chinese mind an influence much greater than the whole bulk of the classics. Notwithstanding their great importance for those who study Chinese thought, they have been completely left aside. In fact, the whole of real Chinese literature is still unknown to the Westerners.

It is a pity that it should be so. The novels and stories throw an extraordinary light on Chinese everyday life that foreigners have been very seldom, and now will never be, able to witness, and they illustrate in a striking way the idea the Chinese have formed of the other world. One is able at last to understand what is the meaning of the *huen* or superior soul, which leaves the body after death or during sleep, but keeps its outward appearance and ordinary clothes; the *p'aï* or inferior soul which remains in the decaying body, and sometimes is strong enough to prevent it from decaying, and to give it all the appearancesof life. The magicians of the Tao religion, or Taoist priests, play a great part in these stories, and the Buddhist ideas of metempsychosis give the opportunity of more complicated situations than we dream of.

Among the most celebrated works, I have chosen the "Strange Stories from the Lodge of Leisures," *Leao chai Chi yi*. It was written in the second half of the eighteenth century by P'ou Song-lin (P'ou Lieou-hsien), of Tsy-cheou, in the Chantong province.

The whole work is composed of more than three hundred stories. I have selected twenty-five among the most characteristic.

This being a literary work, and having nothing scientific to boast of, I have tried to give my English readers the same literary impression that the Chinese has. *Tradutore traditore*, say the Italians; I hope I have not been too much of a traitor.

A translation is always a most difficult work; if it is materially exact, word for word and sentence by sentence, the so-called scientific men are satisfied, but all the charm, beauty, and interest of the original are lost. Very often, too, such translation is obscure and unintelligible. Each nation has an heirloom of traditions, customs, or religion to which its literature constantly refers. If the reader is not acquainted with that literature, these references will convey no meaning to his mind, or they may even convey a false one. In Chinese, this difficulty is greater than in any other language; the Far Eastern civilisation has had a development of its own, and its legends and superstitions have nothing in common with the Western folklore. The Chinese mind is radically different from ours, and has grown, in every generation, more different by reason of a different training and a different ideal in life. The Chinese writing, moreover, has strengthened those differences; it represents the ideasthemselves, instead of representing the words; each Chinese sign may be rightly translated by either of the three or more words by which our language analytically describes every aspect of one same idea. The sign which is read *Tao*, for instance, must be, according to the sentence, translated by any of the words: direction, rule, doctrine, religion, way, road, word, verb; all of them being the different forms of the same idea of direction, moral or physical.

Some French sinologists, aware of this difficulty, now translate the texts literally, and try to explain the meaning by a number of notes, which sometimes leave only one or two lines of text in a page. This method seems at first more scientific; it explains everything in the most careful way, and is very useful for the translation of inscriptions or of certain obscure passages in historical books. But for real literature, it is the greatest possible error, leaving out, as it does, all the impression and illusion the author intended to convey. Besides, the necessity of going, at every word, down the page in order to find the meaning in a note, tires the reader and takes away all the pleasure he should derive from the book.

One may even say that a materially exact translation is, in reality, a false one; the words we use in writing and speaking being mere technical signs by which we represent our ideas. For instance, the word "cathedral" will certainly not convey the same idea to two men, one of whom has only seen St. Paul's, and the other only Notre-Dame de Paris; for the first, cathedral means a dome; for the other it means two towers and a long ogival nave. Below the outward appearance of the words there lie so many different images that it is absolutely necessary to know the mentality of a nation in order to master its language. In fact, a true translation will be the one that, though sometimes materially inexact, will give the reader the same impression he would have if he were reading the original text.

Since I first went to China, in 1901, I have had many opportunities of acquainting myself with all the superstitions of the lower classes, with all the splendid mental and intellectual training of the learned. My experience has helped me to perceive what was hidden beneath the words; and in my translation I have sometimes supplied what the author only thought necessary to imply. In many places the translation is literal; in other places it is literary, it being impossible for a Western writer to retain all the long and useless talking, all the repetitions that Chinese writing and Chinese taste are equally fond of.

GEORGE SOULIÉ.

THE GHOST IN LOVE

On the 15th day of the First Moon, in the second year of the period of "Renewed Principles," the streets of the town of the Eastern Lake were thronged with people who were strolling about.

At the setting of the sun every shop was brightly lit up; processions of people moved hither and thither; strings of boys were carrying lanterns of every form and colour; whole families passed, every member of whom, young or old, small or big, was holding at the end of a thin bamboo the lighted image of a bird, an animal, or a flower.

Richer ones, several together, were carrying enormous dragons whose luminous wings waved at every motion and whose glaring eyes rolled from right to left. It was the Fête of the Lanterns.

A young man, clothed in a long pale green dress, allowed himself to be pushed about by the crowd; the passers-by bowed to him:

"How is my Lord Li The-peaceful?"

"The humble student thanks you; and you, how are you?"

"Very well, thanks to your happy influence."

"Does the precious student soon pass his second literary examination?"

"In two months; ignorant that I am. I am idling instead of working."

The fête was drawing to a close when The-peaceful quitted the main street, and went towards the East Gate, where the house was to be found in which he lived alone.

He went farther and farther: the moving lights were rarer; ere long he only saw before him the fire of a white lantern decorated with two red peonies. The paper globe was swinging to the steps of a tiny girl clothed in the blue linen that only slaves wore. The light, behind, showed the elegant silhouette of another woman, this one covered with a long jacket made in a rich pink silk edged with purple.

As the student drew nearer, the belated walker turned round, showing an oval face and big long eyes, wherein shone a bright speck, cruel and mysterious.

Li The-peaceful slackened his pace, following the two strangers, whose small feet glided silently on the shining flagstones of the street.

He was asking himself how he could begin a conversation, when the mistress turned round again, softly smiled, and in a low, rich voice, said to him:

"Is it not strange that in the advancing night we are following the same road?"

"I owe it to the favour of Heaven," he at once replied; "for I am returning to the East Gate; otherwise I should never have dared to follow you."

The conversation, once begun, continued as they walked side by side. The student learned that the pretty walker was called "Double-peony," that she was the daughter of Judge Siu, that she lived out of the city in a garden planted with big trees, on the road to the lake.

On arriving at his house The-peaceful insisted that his new friend should enter and take a cup of tea. She hesitated; then the two young people pushed the door, crossed the small yard bordered right and left with walls covered with tiles, and disappeared in the house....

The servant remained under the portal.

Daylight was breaking when the young girl came out again, calling the servant, who was asleep. The next evening she came again, always accompanied by the slave bearing the white lantern with two red peonies. It was the same each day following.

A neighbour who had watched these nocturnal visits was inquisitive enough to climb the wall which separated his yard from that of the lovers, and to wait, hidden in the shade of the house.

At the accustomed hour the street-door, left ajar, opened to let in the visitors.

Once in the courtyard, they were suddenly transformed, their eyes became flaming and red; their faces grew pale; their teeth seemed to lengthen; an icy mist escaped from their lips.

The neighbour did not see any more: terrified, he let himself slide to the ground and ran to his inner room.

The next morning he went to the student and told him what he had seen. The lover was paralysed with fear: in order to reassure himself he resolved to find out everything he could about his mistress.

He at once went outside the ramparts, on the road to the lake, hoping to find the house of Judge Siu. But at the place he had been told of there was no habitation; on the left, a fallow plain, sown with tombs, went up to the hills; on the right, cultivated fields extended as far as the lake.

However, a small temple was hidden there under big trees. The student had given up all hope; he entered, notwithstanding, into the sacred enclosure, knowing that travellers stayed there sometimes for several weeks.

In the first yard a bonze was passing in his red dress and shaven head; he stopped him.

"Do you know Judge Siu? He has a daughter———"

"Judge Siu's daughter?" asked the priest, astonished. "Well—yes—but wait, I will show her to you."

The-peaceful felt his heart overflowing with joy; his beloved one was living; he was going to see her by the light of day. He quickly followed his companion.

Passing the first court, they crossed a threshold and found themselves in a yard planted with high pine-trees and bordered by a low pavilion. The bonze, passing in first, pushed a door, and, turning round, said:

"Here is Judge Siu's daughter!"

The other stopped, terrified; on a trestle a heavy black lacquered coffin bore this inscription in golden letters: "Coffin of Double-peony, Judge Siu's daughter."

On the wall was an unfolded painting representing the little maid; a white lantern decorated with two red peonies was hung over it.

"Yes, she has been there for the last two years; her parents, according to the rite, are waiting for a favourable day to bury her."

The student silently turned on his heel and went back, not deigning to reply to the mocking bow of the priest.

Evening arrived; he locked himself in, and, covering his head with his blankets, he waited; sleep came to him only at daybreak.

But he could not cease to think of her whom he no longer saw; his heart beat as if to burst, when in the street he perceived the silhouette of a woman which reminded him of his friend.

At last he was incapable of containing himself any longer; one evening he stationed himself behind the door. After a few minutes there was a knock; he opened the door; it was only the little maid:

"My mistress is in tears; why do you never open the door? I come every evening. If you will follow me, perhaps she will forgive you."

The-peaceful, blinded by love, started at once, walking by the light of the white lantern.

The next day the neighbours, seeing that the student's door was open, and that his house was empty, made a declaration to the governor of the town.

The police made an inquest; they collected the evidence of several people who had been watching the nightly visitors the student had received. The bonze of the temple outside the city walls came to say what he knew. The chief of the police went to the road leading to the lake; he crossed the threshold of the little edifice, passed the first yard and at last opened the door of the pavilion.

Everything was in order, but under the lid of the heavy coffin one could see the corner of the long green dress of the student.

In order to do away with evil influences there was a solemn funeral.

Ever since this time, on light clear nights, the passers-by often meet the two lovers entwined together, slowly walking on the road which leads to the lake.

THE FRESCO

In the Great Highway of Eternal Fixity, Mong Flowing-spring and his friend Choo Little-lotus were slowly walking, clothed in the long light green dress of the students.

They had both just passed with success their third literary examination, and were enjoying the pleasures of the capital before returning to their distant province.

As they were both of small means, they were looking now (and at the same time filling their eyes with the movement of the street) for a lodging less expensive than the inn where they had put up on arriving at Pekin.

Leaving the Great Highway, they strolled far into a labyrinth of lanes more and more silent. They soon lost themselves. Undecided, they had stopped, when they spied out the red lacquered portal of a temple of the Mysterious-way.

Pushing the heavy sides of the door, they entered; an old man with his hair tightly drawn together in a black cap, majestic in his grey dress, stood behind the door and appeared to be waiting for them.

"Your coming lightens my humble dwelling," he said in bowing. "I beg you will enter."

"I do not dare! I do not dare!" murmured the two students, bowing in their turn.

They nevertheless entered, crossing the yard on which the portal opened, which was closed, at the end, by the little temple in open woodwork close under the mass of roofs of green tiles.

They went up three steps, then, pushing a narrow and straight door, they entered. In the half-shadow they distinguished on the white altar a statue of Tche Kong The-Supreme-Lord, with a golden face and griffins' feet like the claws of an eagle.

The walls on each side of the altar were painted in frescoes; on the wall on the right you saw goddesses in the midst of flowers. One of these young girls, with a low chignon, was gathering a peony and was slightly smiling. Her mouth, like a cherry, seemed as if it were really opening; one would have sworn that her eyelids fluttered.

Mong Flowing-spring, his eyes fixed on the painting, remained a long time without moving, absorbed in his admiration of the work of art, and disturbed beyond expression by the beauty of the goddess with the low chignon.

"Why is she not living?" said he. "I would willingly give my life for a moment of her love!"

Suddenly he started; the young goddess raised herself upright, bursting with laughter, and got down from the wall. She crossed the door, went down the staircase, stepped over the yard and left the place.

Flowing-spring followed her without reflecting. He saw her going away with a light step, and turn down the first lane; the young student ran behind her.

As he turned the corner, he saw her stop at the entrance of a small house. She was gracefully waving her hand, and, with sly glances, made him signs to come.

He hastened forward and entered in his turn. In the silent house there was nobody, no one but the goddess standing in her long mauve dress and nibbling the flower that she had picked and that she still held in her hand.

"I bow down," said the student, who knelt to salute her.

"Rise! you exceed the rites prescribed," she replied.

"I bend my head, not being able to bear the splendour of your beauty."

As she did not seem to be discontented he continued telling her his admiration and his desire. He approached, touched her hand; she started, but did not draw back. He then took her in his arms; she did not make much resistance.

The moments passed rapidly. They spoke to each other in a low voice, when, suddenly in the street, a noise of heavy boots resounded; steps stopped before the door; the lock was shaken; oaths were heard.

The young girl grew pale; she told Flowing-spring to hide himself under the bed. The student felt his heart become quite small; he crouched down in the shadow, not even being able to breathe. From the depth of his hiding-place, he saw an officer enter, his face in black lacquer, covered with a golden cuirass and surrounded by a troop of young girls in long dresses of bright colours.

"I smell an odour of human flesh!" grumbled the officer, walking heavily and going round the room.

"Hide yourself well!" the goddess murmured to her lover, raising herself from the bed and white with terror. "If you can escape from him, wait till we have left, and open the little door at the end of the garden; then run away quickly!"

"There is a man here! I smell him! He must be delivered to me! If not, I shall punish the person who has hidden him."

"We know nothing!" all the young women said together.

"Very well! Let us go out."

Then, following the gracious troop which the goddess had joined, he crossed the threshold.

Flowing-spring, hidden under the bed, waited till the noise of the boots had gone away. Then he glided with caution from his refuge.

Half bent, listening with anxiety in fear of being surprised, he flew from the room and crossed the garden.

During this time Choo Little-lotus, having remained in the temple, had not remarked the departure of his friend. But, turning round and not any longer seeing him, he questioned the old magician.

"Your friend is not far off," he replied.

Then, showing him the wall, he said:

"Look! here he is!"

And, indeed, in the centre of the fresco, the image of Flowing-spring was painted; he was crouched in among the flowers, straining his ear. The image moved, and, suddenly, the student separated himself from the wall and advanced, looking sad and anxious.

Choo Little-lotus, terrified, was looking at him. The other told him his adventure. As he spoke a terrible clap of thunder was heard. The two friends instinctively shut their eyes; when they opened them, their glance fell on the fresco: the goddesses had taken their places there again, in the midst of the flowers; but the young girl with the low chignon was no longer there.

The magician smiled at Flowing-spring:

"Love has touched her. She has become a woman and is waiting for you in your village."

THE DWARF HUNTERS

The heavy summer in the South is particularly hard to bear for those who are ill. The damp heat keeps them awake, and thousands of insects trouble their rest.

Wang Little-third-one, stretched on his bed made of bamboo laths, where a low fever kept him, complained of it to all those who came to see him, especially to his friend the magician officiating priest of the little temple situated in the neighbouring crossway.

The magician knew something of medicine; he prescribed a calming potion and retired.

When Little-third-one had drunk the potion, his fever fell and he was able to enjoy a little sleep. He was awakened by a slight noise; night had come on; the room was lighted by the full moon, which threw a bright gleam by the open door.

All the insects were moving and flying hither and thither; white ants who gnaw wood, bad-smelling bugs, enormous cockroaches, mosquitoes, innumerable and various flies.

As Little-third-one was looking, his attention was drawn by a movement on the threshold: a small man, not bigger than a thumb, advanced with precautious steps; in his hand he held a bow; a sword was hanging at his side.

Little-third-one, on looking closer, saw two dogs as big as shirt-buttons running before the man with the bow; they suddenly stopped: the archer approached, held out his weapon, and discharged the arrow. A cockroach who was crawling before the dogs made a bound, fell on its back, moved again, then remained motionless; the arrow had run through it.

Behind the first huntsman others had come; some were on horseback, armed with swords; some on foot.

From that time it was a pursuit without intermission; hundreds of insects were shot. At first the mosquitoes escaped; but as they cannot fly for long, every time that one remained still it was transpierced by the huntsmen.

Soon nothing was left of all the insects who broke the silence with their buzzing, their gnashing of teeth, or their falling.

A horseman then was seen galloping over the room, looking from right to left. He then gave the signal; all the huntsmen called their dogs, went towards the door, and disappeared.

Little-third-one had not moved, in order not to disturb the hunt. At last he peacefully went to sleep, henceforth sure of not being awakened by a sting or a bite. He awoke late the next day almost cured.

When his friend the magician came to see him, he told him his experience: the other smiled. Wang understood that the mysterious hunters came from the little temple.

THE CORPSE THE BLOOD-DRINKER

Night was slowly falling in the narrow valley. On the winding path cut in the side of the hill about twenty mules were following each other, bending under their heavy load; the muleteers, being tired, did not cease to hurry forward their animals, abusing them with coarse voices.

Comfortably seated on mules with large pack-saddles, three men were going along at the same pace as the caravan of which they were the masters. Their thick dresses, their fur boots, and their red woollen hoods protected them from the cold wind of the mountain.

In the darkness, rendered thicker by a slight fog, the lights of a village were shining, and soon the mules, hurrying all together, jostling their loads, crowded before the only inn of the place.

The three travellers, happy to be able to rest, got down from their saddles when the innkeeper came out on the step of his door and excused himself, saying all his rooms were taken.

"I have still, it is true, a large hall the other side of the street, but it is only a barn, badly shut. I will show it to you."

The merchants, disappointed, consulted each other with a look; but it was too late to continue their way; they followed their landlord.

The hall that was shown to them was big enough and closed at the end by a curtain. Their luggage was brought; the bed-clothes rolled on the pack-saddles were spread out, as usual, on planks and trestles.

The meal was served in the general sitting-room, in the midst of noise, laughing, and movement—smoking rice, vegetables preserved in vinegar, and lukewarm wine served in small cups. Then every one went to bed; the lights were put out and profound silence prevailed in the sleeping village.

However, towards the hour of the Rat, a sensation of cold and uneasiness awoke one of the three travellers named Wang Fou, Happiness-of-the-kings. He turned in his bed, but the snoring of his two companions annoyed him; he could not get to sleep. Again, seeing that his rest was finished, he got up, relit the lamp which was out, took a book from his baggage, and stretched himself out again. But if he could not sleep, it was just as impossible to read. In spite of himself, his eyes quitted the columns of letters laid out in lines and searched into the darkness that the feeble light did not contrive to break through.

A growing terror froze him. He would have liked to awaken his companions, but the fear of being made fun of prevented him.

By dint of looking, he at last saw a slight movement shake the big curtain which closed the room. There came from behind a crackling of wood being broken. Then a long, painful threatening silence began again.

The merchant felt his flesh thrill; he was filled with horror, in spite of his efforts to be reasonable.

He had put aside his book, and, the coverlet drawn up to his nose, he fixed his enlarged eyes on the shadowy corners at the end of the room.

The side of the curtain was lifted; a pale hand held the folds. The stuff, thus raised, permitted a being to pass, whose form, hardly distinct, seemed penetrated by the shadow.

Happiness-of-kings would have liked to scream; his contracted throat allowed no sound to escape. Motionless and speechless, he followed with his horrified look the slow movement of the apparition which approached.

He, little by little, recognised the silhouette of a female, seen by her short quilted dress and her long narrow jacket. Behind the body he perceived the curtain again moving.

The spectre, in the meantime bending over the bed of one of the sleeping travellers, appeared to give him a long kiss.

Then it went towards the couch of the second merchant. Happiness-of-kings distinctly saw the pale figure, the eyes, from which a red flame was shining, and sharp teeth, half-exposed in a ferocious smile, which opened and shut by turns on the throat of the sleeper.

A start disturbed the body under the cover, then all stopped: the spectre was drinking in long draughts.

Happiness-of-kings, seeing that his turn was coming, had just strength enough to pull the coverlet over his head. He heard grumblings; a freezing breath penetrated through the wadded material.

The paroxysm of terror gave the merchant full possession of his strength; with a convulsive movement he threw his coverlet on the apparition, jumped out of his bed, and, yelling like a wild beast, he ran as far as the door and flew away in the night.

Still running, he felt the freezing breath in his back, he heard the furious growlings of the spectre.

The prolonged howling of the unhappy man filled the narrow street and awoke all the sleepers in their beds, but none of them moved; they hid themselves farther and farther under their coverlets. These inhuman cries meant nothing good for those who should have been bold enough to go outside.

The bewildered fugitive crossed the village, going faster and faster. Arriving at the last houses, he was only a few feet in advance and felt himself fainting.

The road at the extremity of the village was bordered with narrow fields shaded with big trees. The instinct of a hunted animal drove on the distracted merchant; he made a brisk turn to the right, then to the left, and threw himself behind the knotted trunk of a huge chestnut-tree. The freezing hand already touched his shoulder; he fell senseless.

In the morning, in broad daylight, two men who came to plough in this same field were surprised to perceive against the tree a white form, and, on the ground, a man stretched out. This fact coming after the howling in the night appeared strange to them; they turned back and went to find the Chief of the Elders. When they returned, the greater part of the inhabitants of the village followed them.

They approached and found that the form against the tree was the corpse of a young woman, her nails buried in the bark; from her mouth a stream of blood had flowed and stained her white silk jacket. A shudder of horror shook the lookers-on: the Chief of the Elders recognised his daughter dead for the last six months whose coffin was placed in a barn, waiting for the burial, a favourable day to be fixed by the astrologers.

The innkeeper recognised one of his guests in the man stretched on the ground, whom no care could revive.

They returned in haste to find out in what condition the coffin was: the door of the barn was still open. They went in; a coverlet was thrown on the ground near the entrance; on two beds the great sun lit up the hollow and greenish aspect of the corpses whose blood had been emptied.

Behind the drawn curtain the coffin was found open. The corpse of the young woman evidently had not lost its inferior soul, the vital breath. Like all beings deprived of conscience and reason, her ferocity was eager for blood.

LOVE REWARDED

Lost in the heart of Peking, in one of the most peaceful neighbourhoods of the Yellow City, the street of Glowing-happiness was sleeping in the silence and in the light.

On the right and left of the dusty road was some waste ground, where several red mangy, and surly dogs were sleeping. Five or six low houses, their white walls forming a line not well defined, whose low roofs were covered with grey tiles, bordered the road.

In the first year of the Glorious-Strength, four hundred years ago, a young man with long hair tied together under the black gauze cap of the scholars, clothed in a pink dress with purple flowers, was walking in the setting sun, stepping cautiously in order not to cover with dust his shoes with thick felt soles.

When the first stars began to shine in the darkening sky, he entered one of the houses. A wick in a saucer, soaking in oil, burning and smoking, vaguely lighted an open book on the table: one could only guess, in the shadow, the form of a chair, a bed in a corner, and a few inscriptions hanging on the whitewashed walls.

The scholar seated himself before his table and resumed, as he did every evening, his reading of the Classics, of which he sought to penetrate the entire meaning. Late passers-by in this lonely thoroughfare still saw his lamp shining across the trellises of the windows far into the night.

Golden-dragon lived alone. Now, on that evening an inexplicable languor made him dreamy; his eyes followed in vain the text; his rebellious thoughts were scattered.

Impatiently at last he was just going to put out his lamp and go to bed, when he heard some one knocking at the door.

"Come in!" he cried.

The door grinding on its hinges, a young woman appeared clothed in a long gown of bright green silk, gracefully lifting her foot to cross the threshold, and bowing with her two hands united. Golden-dragon, hurriedly rising to reply, waved in his turn his fists joined together at the same height as his visage and said, according to the ritual: "Be kind enough to be seated! What is your noble name?" The visitor did not pronounce a word; her large black eyes, shadowed by long eyelashes, were fixed on the face of her host, while she tried to regain her panting breath.

As she advanced, Golden-dragon felt a strange feeling of admiration and love.

He did not think such a perfect beauty could exist. As he remained speechless, she smiled, and her smile had on him the effect of a strong drink on a hungry man; troubled and dazed, he lost the conscience of his personality and his acts.

The next morning the sun was shining when he awoke, asking himself if he had not been dreaming. He thought all day long of his strange visitor, making thousands of suppositions.

Evening coming on, she suddenly entered, and it was as it had been the night before.

Two months passed; then the young girl's visits abruptly ceased. The night covered everything with its black veil, but nobody appeared at the door. Golden-dragon the first night, waited for her till the hour of the Rat; at last he went to his couch and fell asleep. Almost immediately he saw her carried away by two horny *yecha*; she was calling him:

"My beloved, I am drawn away towards the inferior regions. I shall never be able to get away if prayers are not said for me. My body lies in the next house."

He started out of sleep in the efforts he made to fly to her, and could not rest again in his impatience to assert what she had said.

As soon as the sun was up, he ran towards the only house that was next to his. He knocked; no one replied. Pushing the door, he entered. The house seemed to be recently abandoned, the rooms were empty, but in a side hall a black lacquered coffin rested on trestles; on a table the "Book of Liberation" was open at the chapter of "The great recall."

Golden-dragon doubted no longer; he sang in a high voice the entire chapter, shut the book, and returned home full of a strange peacefulness.

Every evening from that time, at the hour when she had appeared to him, he lit a lantern, went to the house next door and read a chapter of the holy text.

Years passed by; he got beyond his fiftieth year, grew bent, and walked with difficulty, but he never missed performing the duty he had imposed on himself for his unknown friend.

The house where the coffin was placed had successively been let to several families; but he had arranged that the funereal room should never be touched. The lodgers bowed to the scholar when he came, and talked to him; the whole town was entertained with this touching example of such everlasting love.

"So much constancy and such fidelity cannot remain without reward," they said.

But time slipped by and nothing came to change the regular life of the old man.

On his seventieth birthday, as he went to his neighbours, he remarked a violent excitement.

"My wife has just had a child," said the chief of the family, going to meet him. "Come and wish her happiness; she does not cease to ask for you."

"Is it a boy?"

"No, unhappily, a girl, but such a pretty little thing."

Followed by the happy father, the scholar with white hair penetrated into the room; the mother smiled, holding out the baby to him. Golden-dragon suddenly started; the child held out her arms to him and on her little lips, hardly formed, hovered the shadow of a disappeared smile, the smile of the unknown woman.

And as he looked an extraordinary sensation troubled him; he felt he was growing younger, more vigorous. Soon, in the midst of the cries of admiration of the whole family, the bent old man grew straight again; his grey hair turned black, and the change continued; he became a young man, a boy, and soon a child.

When the Bell of the great Tower struck the hour of the Rat, he was a fat pink baby playing and laughing with the little girl.

The governor of the town, being informed, personally directed an inquiry. It was discovered that the coffin had disappeared at the same hour when the transformation had happened.

The Emperor, on the report of the governor, ordered the two children to receive a handsome dowry.

As to them, they grew up, loved each other, and lived happy and well as far as the limits of human longevity.

THE WOMAN IN GREEN

At this time, in the Pavilion-of-the-guests, in the Monastery-of-the-healing-springs, the most celebrated of the Fo-kien province, lived a young scholar whose name was Little-cypress.

As soon as the sun rose he was at his work, seated near the trellised window. When night fell, his lamp still lit the outline of the wooden trellis.

One morning a shadow darkened his book; he raised his eyes: a young woman with a long green skirt, her face of matchless beauty, was standing outside the window and was looking at him.

"You are then always working, Lord Little-cypress?" she said.

She was so bewitching that he knew her immediately for a goddess; but all the same he asked her where she lived and what was her name.

"Your lordship has looked on his humble wife; he has known her as a goddess. What is the use of so many questions?"

Little-cypress, satisfied with this reply, invited her to enter the house. She came in; her waist was so small, one would almost have thought that her body was divided in two.

He invited her to sit down; they talked and laughed together a long time.

He asked her to sing, and, with a low voice, which filled her friend with rapture, she sang:

> "On the trees the bird pursues his companion; Oppressed slaves free themselves with love. How has my Lord lived alone, Without enjoying all the pleasures of married life?"

The sound vibrated like a thread of silk; it penetrated the ear and troubled the heart. As she finished, she suddenly arose.

"A man is standing near the window, he is listening to us ... he is going round ... he is trying to see."

"Since when does a goddess fear a man?" replied Little-cypress, laughing.

"I am troubled without knowing why; my heart beats. I wish to go."

She went to open the door, but abruptly shut it.

"I do not know why I am thus upset. Will you accompany me as far as the entrance gate?"

Little-cypress held her up till they got to the gate; he had just left her and turned his head, when he heard her call for help in a voice full of anguish. He hurriedly turned round; no one was to be seen.

As he was looking for her with stupefaction his eyes fell on a big cobweb, stretched in the corner of the wall. The ugly and gigantic insect held in its claws a dragon-fly who was struggling and dolefully crying. Affected by this sight, he hastened to deliver it.

The pretty insect immediately flew in the direction of the Pavilion-of-the-guests. Little-cypress saw it go in at the window and alight on the stone for grinding the ink.

Then it arose again and alighted on the paper which was placed on the table; there it oddly crawled, retracing its steps, returning, advancing, and stopping. After a moment it took its flight and disappeared in the sky.

Little-cypress, much puzzled, approached and looked; on the paper was written in big strokes the word "Thanks."

THE FAULT AND ITS CONSEQUENCES

When Dawning-colour was on the point of dying, he called his mother to him.

"Mother," he said, "I am going to die. I do not wish White-orchid, my young wife, to feel herself bound to keep the widowhood. When her mourning will be finished, she will marry again: our son is only three years old; you will keep him with you."

Now, the mourning was not yet finished and the coffin was still in the house waiting for a favourable day, when the young widow began to find the solitude weigh upon her.

A rich sluggard of the village, named Adolescent, had several times sent proposals to her through a neighbour; she at last was unwise enough to agree to an interview with him. When evening came, Adolescent jumped over the neighbour's wall and went to her room.

He had not been there half an hour when there arose a great noise in the hall where the coffin was; it seemed as if the cover was violently thrown to the ground. A little slave who was called afterwards as a witness told how she ran into the yard and saw her master's corpse brandishing a sword and jumping towards the room where the lovers were to be found.

A few instants after, she saw the young widow come out screaming and run to the garden. Adolescent followed her, covered with blood; he crossed the threshold and disappeared in the night.

Now, Adolescent, flying from danger, pushed the first door that he came across in the street; it was that of a young couple; the husband, named Wang, was absent and only expected to return the next day. The young wife, hearing a noise, thought it was her husband returning.

"Is that you?" she asked, without quite waking up.

Adolescent, who knew Madame Wang was pretty, answered "Yes" in a low voice, taking advantage of her error.

A short time after, at Wang's turn to enter, he struck a light, saw a man in his room, and, furious, seized a pike. Adolescent tried to hide himself under the bed, but the husband transpierced him several times. He wished to kill his wife, but she so much begged him not to that he spared her.

The cries and supplications which came from the room had, however, awoke the neighbours, who came in; they pulled Adolescent's body from under the bed; he died almost directly.

There was a silence; the affair was serious. Then one of the assistants said:

"The judges won't believe that you were in your right of outraged husband; you ought to have killed your wife also. As it is, you will be condemned."

Thereupon, Wang killed the unhappy woman.

During this time Dawning-colour's mother, having heard the screams of her daughter-in-law, thought there was a burglar in the house; she cried for help and tried to light a lamp, but she was trembling, and her curtains caught fire.

Some neighbours arrived in haste; while a few of them extinguished the fire, the others, armed with crossbows, ran through the house and garden in search of the thief.

At the bottom of the orchard they saw a white mass moving at the foot of the wall. Without waiting to ascertain what it was, they shot several arrows; everything was still. The archers approached and lit a torch; they saw the body of White-orchid transpierced in the head and chest.

Horrified by what they had done, they informed the old woman, who said nothing.

But this was not all. The elder brother of White-orchid, furious at the tragic death of his sister, had a lawsuit with the archers and the old woman.

As usual, the judges ruined both parties; they condemned Dawning-colour's mother and the archers to receive five hundred bamboo strokes. The latter were not strong enough to bear this punishment, and died under the stick. And thus the affair ended.

DECEIVING SHADOWS

Night was falling when the horseshoes of the mules of my caravan resounded on the slippery flagstones of the village.

Tired by a long day of walking, I directed my steps towards the large hall of the inn, with the intention of resting a moment while my repast was being prepared.

In the darkened room the glimmer of a small opium-lamp lit up the pale and hollow face of an old man, occupied in holding over the flame a small ball of the black drug, which would soon be transformed into smoke, source of forgetfulness and dreams.

The old man returned my greeting, and invited me to lie down on the couch opposite to him. He handed me a pipe already prepared and we began talking together. As ordered by the laws of politeness, I remarked to my neighbour that he seemed robust for his age.

"My age? Do you, then, think I am so old?"

"But, as you are so wise, you must have seen sixty harvests?"

"Sixty! I am not yet thirty years old! But you must have come from a long way off, not to know who I am."

And while rolling the balls with dexterity in the palm of his hand, and making them puff out to the heat of the lamp, he told me his story.

His name was Liu Favour-of-heaven. Born and brought up in the capital, he had been promoted six years before to the post of sub-prefect in the town on which our refuge was dependent.

When coming to take his post, he stopped at the inn, the same one where we were. The house was full; but he had remarked, on entering, a long pavilion which seemed uninhabited. The landlord, being asked, looked perplexed; he ended by saying that the pavilion had been shut for the last two years; all the travellers had complained of noises and strange visions; probably mischievous spirits lived there.

Favour-of-heaven, having lived in the capital, but little believed in phantoms. He found the occasion excellent to establish his reputation in braving imaginary dangers.

His wife and his children implored him in vain; he persisted in his intention of remaining the night alone in the haunted house.

He had lights brought; installed himself in a big armchair, and placed across his knees a long and heavy sword.

Hours passed by; the sonorous noise of the gong struck by the watchman announced successively the hours, first of the Pig, then of the Rat. He grew drowsy. Suddenly, he was awakened by the gnashing of teeth. All the lights were out; the darkness, however, was not deep enough to prevent his being able to distinguish everything confusedly. Anguish seized him; his heart beat with violence; his staring eyes were fixed on the door.

By the half-opened door he perceived a round white mass, the deformed head of a monster, who, appearing little by little, stretched long hands with twisted fingers and claws.

Favour-of-heaven mechanically raised his weapon; his blood frozen in his veins, he tried to strike the head, whose indistinct features were certainly dreadful. Without doubt the blow had struck, for a frightful cry was heard; all the demons of the inferior regions seemed let loose with this yell; calls were heard from all sides. The trellised frames of the windows were shaken with violence. The monster gained the door. Favour-of-heaven pursued him and threw him down.

His terror was such that he felt he must strike and kill. Hardly had he finished than there entered, rolling from side to side, a little being, quite round, brandishing unknown weapons at the end of innumerable small hands. The prefect, with one blow, cut him in two like a watermelon.

However, the windows were shaken with growing rage; unknown beings entered by the door without interruption; the prefect threw them down one after another: a black shadow first, then a head balancing itself at the end of a huge neck, then the jaw of a crocodile, then a big bird with the chest and feet of a donkey.

Trembling all over, the man struck right and left, exhausted and panting; a cold perspiration overwhelmed him; he felt his strength gradually giving way, when the cock crowed at last the coming of the day.

Little by little, grey dawn designed the trellis of the windows, then the sun suddenly appeared above the horizon and darted its rays across the rents in the paper.

Favour-of-heaven felt his heart stand still; on the floor inundated with blood, the bodies lying there had human forms, forms that he knew: this one looked like his second wife, and this one, this little head that had rolled against the foot of the table, he would have sworn that it was his last son.

With a mad cry he threw away his weapon and ran to open the door, through which the sun poured in.

An armed crowd was moving in the yard.

"My family! my family! where is my family?"

"They are all with you in the pavilion!"

But as they were speaking they saw with stupor the hair of the young man becoming white, and the wrinkles of age cover his face, while he remained motionless as well as insensible.

They drew near; he rolled fainting on the ground. "And thus," ended the sub-prefect in the silence of the dark hall, where only the little light of the opium-lamp was shining, "I remained several days without knowledge of anything. When I came to myself, I had to bear the sorrow of having killed my whole family in these atrocious circumstances. I resigned my post: I had magnificent tombs built for all those who were killed this fatal night, and, since then, I smoke without ceasing the agreeable drug, in order to fly away from the remembrance, which will haunt me until my last day."

PEACEFUL-LIGHT

In the time when the Shining Dynasty had just conquered the throne, the eastern coasts of the Empire were ravaged by the rapid junks commanded by the cruel inhabitants of the Japanese islands, the irresistible *Wo tsz*.

Now, it happened that the *Wo tsz* Emperor lost his first wife; knowing the beauty of Chinese women, he charged one of his officers to bring back some of them.

The officer, at the head of a numerous troop, landed not far from the town of The-Smoky-wall. No resistance was possible; the population was given the example of flight by the functionaries, at least it was thus said in the Annals of the prefecture.

The country being far from the big centres, the women were not great coquettes; only one, named Peaceful-light, had always been careful, since childhood, not to allow her feet to become naturally large; they were constantly bound up, so much so that she could hardly walk.

Her large soft eyes were shaded with heavy eyelashes; one of the literati of the place took delight in quoting the poets of antiquity on them:

> Under the willow of her eyelashes The tranquil river of her eyes shines forth. I bend and see my image reflected in them. Could she be deceitful like the deep water?

When the pirates were coming, she begged her family to leave her, and to fly without the risk of being delayed by her.

"It is the just punishment for my coquetry," she told them. "Fear nothing for me, however. I am going to take a strong dose of the paste extracted from the flowers of Nao-yang which makes one sleep. The pirates will think I am dead, and will leave me."

The family allowed themselves to be persuaded, and departed. As to Peaceful-light, she was asleep almost directly after taking the drug, and she remained motionless on her bed.

The pirates, entering everywhere, at last arrived in the house and remained struck with admiration by her beauty. The officer who was called, at first thought her dead and was much grieved, but, touching her hand and finding it warm and limp, he resolved to carry her away.

When the ravishers were re-embarked, the strong sea-air and the motion of the boat revived the young girl; she awoke, and was horrified to find herself surrounded by strangers. The one who seemed the chief spoke to her in Chinese language in order to reassure her:

"Fear nothing. No harm will come to you. On the contrary, the highest destiny awaits you; my Lord The Emperor designs you to the honour of his couch."

Seeing that no one troubled her, Peaceful-light was reassured; she resolved to wait, confident in her destiny, and knowing that she had still, ready in her sleeve, in case of necessity, a narcotic dose strong enough to kill her.

As soon as she landed, she was taken in great haste to the Palace. The Emperor, greatly satisfied with her beauty, conferred on her at once the rank of first favourite.

But all the luxury and love which surrounded her could not make her forget her family and her country; she resolved to run away.

In order to manage it, she complained to her master how sad it was for her never to be able to speak her own language with companions from her country. The Emperor, happy to be able to please her, gave orders to fit out a sea-junk, in order to go to the Chinese coast.

The day when all was ready the young girl found means of pouring into her master's drink a dose of her narcotic. Then, when he was asleep, she took his private seal and, going out of the room, she called the intendant of the Palace and said to him:

"The Emperor has ordered me to go to China to fetch a magician, a member of my family, who has great power on water and wind. Here is the seal, proof of my mission. The ship must be almost ready."

The intendant knew that a junk had been specially prepared to go to China; he saw the seal; what suspicion could he have? He had a palanquin brought as quickly as possible; two hours after, the wood of the junk groaned under the blows of the unfurling waves.

Arriving in sight of the coast, on the pretext of not frightening the population, the young girl begged the officer who accompanied her to send a messenger to the prefect of the town, bearing a letter that she had prepared. The officer, without distrust, sent one of his men.

The letter of Peaceful-light showed a whole scheme to which the prefect could but give his consent. The messenger returned, bringing to the officer and to the men an invitation to take part in the feast that was being prepared for them, their intentions not being bad.

Peaceful-light retired into her family, who welcomed her with a thousand demonstrations of joy.

In the wine that was freely poured out for the strangers they had dissolved the flowers of Nao-yang. The effects were not long in being felt; a torpor that they attributed to the table excesses seized them one after another. They were soon all sleeping deeply. Men arrived with swords, glided near them, and, a signal being given, cut off their heads.

While these events were passing in China, others still more serious were happening in Japan. Soon after the departure of Peaceful-light, the Emperor's brother penetrated into the room where the sovereign was left sleeping. This brother was ambitious; he profited by the occasion, killed the unhappy Mikado, took possession of the seals of the State, and, calling his partisans in haste, proclaimed himself Chief of the State. Only a part of the princes followed him; the others, filled with indignation by the crime that had been accomplished, united their troops to crush the usurper; civil war tore the whole of Japan to pieces.

As to Peaceful-light, by order of the authorities she received public congratulations and gifts of land which allowed her to marry and be happy, as she merited.

HONG THE CURRIER

"In the time when the Justice of Heaven was actively employed with the affairs of the earth, one of my ancestors had an adventure to which we owe our present fortune, and of which few men of to-day have seen the equal."

Thus began my friend Hong; reclining on the red cushions of the big couch, he fanned himself gracefully with an ivory fan painted all over.

"Our family, as you know, originally came from the town of The-Black-chain in the province of The-Foaming-rivers. Our ancestor Hong The-just was a currier by trade; he cut and scraped the skins that were entrusted to him. His family was composed only of his wife, who helped him as well as she could.

"Notwithstanding this persistent labour, they were very poor; no furniture ornamented the three rooms in the small house that they hired in the Street-of-the-golden-flowers.

"When the last days of the twelfth moon in that year arrived, they found they were owing six strings of copper cash to ten different creditors. With all they possessed, there only remained 400 cash. What were they to do? They reflected for a long time. Hong The-just at last said to his wife:

"'Take these 400 cash; you will be able to buy rice to live on. As to me, as I cannot pay my debts before the first day of the first moon, I am going to leave the town and hide myself in the mountain. My creditors, not seeing me, will believe you when you tell them that I have been to find money in the neighbouring town. Once the first day of the first moon passed, as law ordains to wait till the following term, I shall then come back, and we shall continue to live as well as we can.'

"It was indeed the wisest thing to do. His wife made him a parcel of a blanket and a few dry biscuits. She wept at seeing him go away quite bent, walking with difficulty on the slippery flagstones of the street.

"The snow was falling in thick flakes and already covered the grey tiled roofs, when Hong The-just left the city gate and directed his steps to a cave that he knew of in a lonely valley.

"He arrived at last, and, throwing his heavy load on the ground, he glanced around him in order to choose the place where he would sleep.

"An exclamation of stupor escaped from him when he saw, seated motionless on a stone, a man clothed in a long sable cloak, with a cap of the same fur, looking at him in a mournful, indifferent way.

"'How strange!' at last said Hong, laughing. 'Dare I ask your noble name and the reason that brings you to this remote refuge? How is it that you are not with your friends, drinking hot wine and rejoicing in the midst of the luxuriance of the tables covered with various eatables and brilliant lights?'

"'My name is Yang Glow-of-dawn. And you, what is your precious name?' replied mechanically the first occupant.

"'I am called Hong The-just, and I am here to escape from my creditors.'

"'You, also?' sneered Glow-of-dawn. 'The strokes of Fate do not vary much. As for me, I deal in European goods; my correspondents have not settled my accounts and I am in want of nearly a hundred thousand ounces of silver to close the year. None of my friends could advance me the sum, and here I am, obliged to fly away from my creditors.'

"'A hundred thousand ounces!' cried The-just. 'With a sum like that I should pass the rest of my days in plenty. Anyhow, struck by the same misfortune, we are thus united; let us try to pass cheerfully the last day of the year, and attempt to imagine that these humble cakes are refined food.'

"When they were eating their pastry and drinking water from the near torrent, Glow-of-dawn suddenly said:

"'But you, how much do you owe? I have here a few ounces of silver; maybe you could balance your accounts with them.'

"'My debts do not exceed six strings of copper cash. But how could I dare accept your offer?'

"'Not at all! take these ten ounces; you will pay your debts and bring me here food and wine; that will help me to wait till the end of the festivals.'

"The-just, reiterating his thanks, took the ingots that were offered him and went down as quickly as possible towards the town.

"His wife, on seeing him and hearing his story, could not restrain her joy. She hurried to go and buy provisions of all kinds. Her husband tried to light the stove, but they had not lit a fire for a long time; he found the chimney filled with soot and dust.

"Hong tried to sweep it with a big broom, but the masonry gave way, filling the room with the bricks and rubbish.

"'How very annoying!' grumbled the currier. 'Now the stove is destroyed let us take away what remains, and we will make the fire beneath the opening in the roof!'

"When his wife returned, he was still working. She put down her basket and helped to raise a huge stone that formed the bottom of the hearth. What was their astonishment in seeing a chest, half-broken, from which big ingots of gold were falling!

"'What are we to do with this?' said his wife. 'If we sell this gold, everybody will think that we have stolen it, and we shall be put in prison.'

"'We have only one thing to do,' replied Hong. 'Let us entrust our fortune to my companion in the cave; he is a good man. We shall save him, and he will make our money prosper; I will hurry and tell him.'

"When Hong arrived, it was nearly nightfall; Yang was standing under flakes of snow at the entrance of the grotto; he received him with reproaches:

"'You have come so late that my eyes are sore in looking out for you in vain!'

"'Do not abuse me, Old Uncle; drink this wine and eat these cakes that are still warm, and I will tell you what delayed me.'

"And while Glow-of-dawn ate and drank, the other told him of his adventure and of his intentions about the treasure.

"Surprised and touched, the merchant did not know how to express his wonder and gratitude. They talked over the best way of proceeding to bring the gold and settle the business.

"Then, by the glimmer of a bad lantern, they returned to the town and entered the merchant's house. There the currier washed himself, did his hair, and clothed himself in rich garments. A sedan-chair was waiting for him, followed by sturdy servants; he went away....

"The next day Glow-of-dawn's creditors presented themselves at the house of their debtor. He was standing at the entrance, and bowed in wishing them a thousand times happiness. They entered; tea was brought in by busy servants. They at last discussed the settlement of their yearly accounts. The master of the house found out that he owed 180,000 ounces of silver.

"'We have been informed that larger sums of silver are due to you, but you know the custom; you must settle everything to-day. In order to save you, we are content to make an estimate of your wealth, your goods and lands.'

"'Do not give yourselves such a trouble,' replied the merchant, laughing and waving his hand. 'I thought you would be relentless, so I have been to speak to my elder brother, who has an immense fortune; he has put at my disposal several hundred thousand ounces. But here! I hear the cry of the bearers; it must be him with the chests of white metal.'

"The major domo came hurrying in, carrying high in the air the huge red card with the names and surnames written in black.

"'The venerable Old Great Uncle The-just has arrived!'

"'Allow me?' said Yang, getting up, and going towards the door, of which both sides were open. Hong entered. They made each other a thousand affectionate greetings, as all brothers do who are animated with right feelings.

"'Dear elder brother! here are the gentlemen who have come for the settlement of my accounts about which I spoke to you.'

"'Gentlemen!' and the currier bowed, not without a certain grace that his new fortune had already given him. 'Well! how much is the total amount? I have brought you ten thousand ounces of gold, which is nearly 350,000 ounces of silver. Will you have enough?'

"While he was speaking, bearers were trooping in, and laid down on the ground heavy chests, the lids of which being raised, one could see the bars of precious metal.

"The merchants, thunderstruck by all these riches and generosity, remained silent for a moment; then they bowed low and bade the currier sit in the place of honour.

"Many delicate and exquisite dishes were brought in of which The-just did not even know the names; sweet wines were handed round in small transparent china cups.

"At last the secretaries counted the ingots, and they all returned home paid. When every one had retired, Glow-of-dawn knelt before the currier and, striking the earth with his forehead, he said:

"'Now you are my elder brother. You have rescued me, and I henceforth wish you to live here. My house, my properties, everything I possess belongs to you. Your wife is my sister-in-law.'

"The currier hurried to raise him up and, much moved, said:

"'I do not forget that it is you who saved me when you were still in misfortune. Your good genius has rewarded you. I am only the instrument of Fate.'"

AUTUMN-MOON

In the town of Sou-tcheou a young man lived called Lake-of-the-Immortals; he was wise and generous. His business consisted in going to fetch goods from neighbouring towns, which he afterwards brought back to his native city. He was thus obliged to be absent for lengthy periods, during which he left his house to the care of an elder brother, a celebrated scholar, who was married, and whom he tenderly loved.

Once he had been by the Grand Canal as far as Chen-kiang; the goods he was going to take not being ready, he waited, and to while away the time he visited the Golden Island, whose temples with yellow-tiled roofs show in the verdure above the yellow water of the river, nearly opposite to the town; he passed the night there, as visitors did usually.

When he had just fallen asleep, he saw in a dream a young girl, fourteen or fifteen years old, her visage regular and pure.

On the second night he had the same dream. Surprised, he awoke; it was no dream; the young girl was there, near to him. At a glance he saw she was no human being; he hastened to get up and, saluting, to ask her the ordinary questions.

"My name is Autumn-moon," she replied. "My father was a celebrated magician. When I died, he worked out my future destiny and wrote it down with powerful incantations; this charm has been put into my coffin, so that the inferior authorities should not make any mistake. It was written that, thirty years after my death, I should be called again to life and marry Lake-of-the-Immortals. There you are, and I have come to know my husband."

As she said the last words she slowly vanished in the night. The next day, as the young man, disturbed and preoccupied by this strange adventure, was sitting in his room, thinking of her, she appeared suddenly before his eyes and said:

"Come quickly! something important for you is going to happen at the prefect's palace. We have not a minute to lose."

Lake-of-the-Immortals questioned her, but she would not answer. Then they both crossed the river and walked as fast as they could up to the yamen.

As they arrived at the gate, four soldiers, dragging a prisoner, were on the point of entering. Lake-of-the-Immortals recognised his elder brother in the person of the prisoner; he drew near, threw himself on his neck, and pressed him to his heart.

"How is it that you are here? why this arrest? And you, soldiers, where do you take him?"

"We have orders: what means this interference?" And they pushed the young man aside. Lake-of-the-Immortals was of a violent temper and had a strong affection for his brother; he could not let him go, and answered to the brutality of the soldiers by such a tempest of thumping and kicking that these honest but prudent soldiers asked no more and fled.

"What have you done?" said Autumn-moon. "Hitting soldiers is serious; we must fly."

And all three, running, arrived at the beach, jumped into a small boat, and rowed with all their strength.

When day appeared, they were safely lodged in a small inn, several lis from Chen-kiang. Lake-of-the-Immortals, exhausted, went to sleep immediately. When he awoke, his two companions had disappeared. He asked the innkeeper; nobody had seen them go out.

Distressed and sad, the young man did not dare to show himself outside. He remained solitary in his room. When twilight came, his door opened and a woman entered:

"I bring you a message from Autumn-moon; she has been arrested. If you wish to see her, you must follow me; I will show you the way."

"And my brother? do you know anything?"

"Your brother is safe in Sou-tcheou now. But come and follow me."

They started and soon arrived before a wall, which they got over by helping one another. Through a window giving on the yard they fell in, the lover perceived Autumn-moon on a bed. Two soldiers were trying to tease her, saying:

"What is the use of resisting us, as you will be executed to-morrow morning?"

Lake-of-the-Immortals did not hear any more; he rushed into the room, threw himself on the soldiers, tore a sword from them, and laid them on the ground. Before the wretched men had time to make a gesture of defence, he carried away the girl and flew.

At this moment he started violently, and found himself in his same room in the Golden Island. A servant entered, bringing the breakfast he had ordered when arriving for the first time, the night before, on the island.

As he was asking himself the meaning of such a vivid dream, he heard a noise in the courtyard. Going out, he saw several men surrounding the body of a girl stretched before his door.

"Where does she come from?" asked some one.

"We have never seen her!" said another.

Lake-of-the-Immortals came nearer; it was the body, seemingly senseless, of Autumn-moon. He had her brought immediately into his room. A doctor who had been called declared she was still alive, but needed very careful nursing.

When she awoke at last she smiled feebly to the young man.

"No, it is no dream," she replied to his questions. "Your brother was called before the King of Hells; you saved him. You have saved me also from eternal disappearance, and I am called again to life; the prediction of my father was true."

A fortnight later she was able to get up; they started together and arrived safely at Sou-tcheou. When they got to his brother's house, his sister-in-law told them there had been illness in the house; her husband had been in grave danger of death; he was quite well now.

When they were all together, Lake-of-the-Immortals told what he had seen and done. They all listened to him in silence. The family henceforth lived united and happy.

THE PRINCESS NELUMBO

Gleam-of-day was sleeping; his round face and high forehead denoted the scholar's right intelligence.

All of a sudden he saw a man standing before his bed who appeared to be waiting.

"What is it?" inquired the sleeper, getting up.

"The prince is asking for you."

"Which prince?"

"The prince of the neighbouring territory."

Gleam-of-day, grumbling, got up, put on his court dress and followed his guide. Palanquins were waiting; they started rapidly, and their retinue was soon passing in the midst of innumerable pavilions and towers with pointed roofs.

They at last stopped in the courtyard of the palace; young girls with bright clothing were seen, and looked inquiringly at the new-comer, who was announced with great pomp.

At last Gleam-of-day reached the audience hall. The prince was seated on the throne; he descended the steps and welcomed his guest according to the rites.

"You perfume this neighbourhood," he said. "Your reputation has come to me, and I wished to know you."

The servants brought wine; they began to converse nobly and brilliantly. At last the prince asked:

"Among the flowers, tell me which one you prefer."

"The nelumbo," he replied, without hesitating.

"The nelumbo? it is precisely my daughter's surname. What a curious coincidence! The princess must absolutely know you."

And he made a sign to one of the attendants, who at once went out. A few minutes after, the princess appeared. She was between sixteen and seventeen years old. Nothing could equal her admirable beauty.

Her father ordered her to bow to the scholar and said:

"Here is my daughter Nelumbo."

Gleam-of-day, looking at her, felt troubled to the depth of his soul. The prince spoke to him; he hardly heard, and replied awkwardly. When the princess had retired, the conversation languished; the prince at last rose and put an end to the interview.

During all the way back the young man was ashamed at the same time with his emotion before the girl, as well as his rudeness towards the prince. He was so much troubled that he ordered his retinue to go back to the palace.

When he entered the audience hall, he threw himself to the ground before the prince and begged to be excused for his rudeness.

"You need not excuse yourself; the sentiment that I read in your eyes is powerful and the thought of it is not unpleasant to me."

While Gleam-of-day, happy with this encouragement, was still excusing himself, twenty young girls came running:

"A monster has entered the palace; it is a python ten thousand feet long. It has already devoured thirteen hundred persons; its head is like a mountain peak."

Every one got up; the frightened guard and the courtiers ran hither and thither, looking where they could hide themselves. The princess and her maids-in-waiting were crying for help.

Gleam-of-day at last said to the prince:

"I have only three miserable rooms in a cottage, but you will be safe in them. Will you fly there with your daughter?"

"Let us go as quickly as possible," replied the prince, seizing the princess by the wrist.

They all three ran across the deserted streets. When they arrived, Nelumbo threw herself on the bed, without being able to stop weeping.

Gleam-of-day was so moved that he suddenly awoke: everything was a dream.

Just then he heard a scream in the next room, where his father slept; there was a struggle, blows, and at last a sigh of satisfaction.

The door opened, and the old man was seen pushing an enormous serpent at the end of a stick. When Gleam-of-day turned back to his bed, he found it covered with bees; on the pillow the queen had alighted.

THE TWO BROTHERS

In the town of Sou-tcheou there lived two brothers. The elder, surnamed Merchant, was very rich; the younger, named Deceived-hope, very poor. They lived side by side, and their houses, the paternal inheritance, were only separated by a low wall. They were both married.

This year, the harvest having been bad, Deceived-hope could not afford the necessary rice for his family to live upon. His wife said to him:

"Let us send our son to your brother: he will be touched and will give us something, without any doubt."

Deceived-hope hesitated, but at last decided to take this step which hurt his pride. When the child returned from his uncle's, his hands were empty. They questioned him:

"I told my uncle that you were without rice; he hesitated and looked at my aunt. She then said to me: 'The two brothers live separately; their food also is separate.'"

Deceived-hope and his wife did not say a word; they fetched the bale of rice that was still in their corn-loft and lived thus.

Now, in the town, two or three vagabonds who knew the riches of Merchant broke open his door one night, and tied him up as well as his wife. As he would not show his treasure, they began burning his hands and feet. Merchant and his wife screamed for help. Deceived-hope heard them and got up in order to run to their house, but his wife held him back, and, approaching the wall which separated them, cried:

"The two brothers live separately; their food also is separate."

However, as their cries increased, Deceived-hope could not contain himself, and, seizing a weapon, leapt over the wall, fell on the thieves, and dispersed them. Then, when his brother and his sister-in-law were delivered and quieted, he returned home, saying to his wife:

"They are certain to give us a present."

But, the next day and the days following, they waited in vain! Deceived-hope could not resist the temptation to relate everything to his friends. The same thieves heard of it and, thinking that he would not interfere any more, broke open the door of Merchant the same evening and began again to torture him as well as his wife.

Deceived-hope, indeed, did not wish to interfere. However, his heart and his liver were upset by the painful cries of his brother. He could not forbear running to his help.

The brigands, disconcerted, flew again, but this time Merchant and his wife were severely burnt; they lost the use of their hands and feet.

The next day Merchant said to his wife:

"My brother has saved our lives; without him we should be ruined; I am going to give him a part of what we have."

"Do nothing of the kind," replied his wife; "if he had come sooner, he would have saved our hands and feet; now, thanks to him, we are infirm."

And they did nothing. Deceived-hope, however, wanting money, made an act of sale of his house and sent it to his brother, hoping that he would be touched by his misery and would send back the deed with a present.

In fact Merchant was going to send him some silver ingots, but his wife stopped him:

"Let us take his house; we shall be able to make ours bigger, and it will be much more convenient."

Merchant hesitated a little, but he ended by accepting the act, and sent the price agreed on. Deceived-hope went and settled in another part of the town; with his small capital, he opened a vegetable-shop, which soon prospered.

The brigands, having heard that Merchant was now living alone, broke open his door very quietly, tortured him, and then killed him, taking away all he had. In leaving the place, they cried all over the town:

"Merchant's corn-loft is open! Let all the poor go and take the rice!"

They thus went, one by one, silently, all the poor of the neighbourhood, taking away as much of the heaped-up rice as they could. Soon there was nothing left.

Deceived-hope being informed, wished to revenge his brother; he pursued the brigands and killed two of them.

From this time it was he who every day attended to the needs of his sister-in-law, now in misery. Some months afterwards, exhausted, she died.

Deceived-hope came back and was soon settled in the patrimony that he had recovered. One night he was soundly sleeping, when he saw his brother.

"You have saved us twice, and we have been ungrateful. I should not be dead if I had not acted badly with you. I wish to make amends. Under the stone of the hearth you will find five hundred ounces of gold that I had hidden, and of the existence of which my wife was ignorant."

Deceived-hope started from his sleep; he told his dream to his wife. She at once got up, drew out the stone of the hearth, and found the mass of gold. Henceforth, happy and rich, they lived long and were charitable and friendly with every one.

THE MARBLE ARCH

When the troubles began to break out in Hankow, many families were alarmed. Those who were not ignorant of the powerful organisation of the revolutionists left the town as soon as possible, anticipating that it would soon be plundered and burnt.

The retired prefect, Kiun, was amongst the first to embark in order to go down the river. His house was situated at several lis from the river, on the confines of the suburbs, outside the fortified enclosure. He had only been married a short time, and was living with his father and mother.

When the baggage at last was ready, the bearers fixed it in the middle of their long bamboos and set off two by two, grumbling under the heavy load. The two old people followed; Kiun and his young wife, the charming Seaweed, helped them as well as they could.

In order to avoid crossing the centre of the town, they followed the crenellated wall by an almost deserted road. A young man and woman alone were sauntering in the same direction, carrying parcels on their shoulders.

"Where are you going to?" they asked, as it is the custom to do between travellers.

"As far as the river," replied Kiun. "And you?"

"We also," said the young man. "What is your precious name?"

"My contemptible name is Kiun. But you, deign to inform me about your family?"

"My name is Wang The-king. We are flying from the insurrection."

They thus talked while walking in company.

Seaweed took the advantage of a moment when the new-comers were a little in front to bend towards her husband.

"Do not let us get in the same junk with these strangers. The man has looked at me several times in a rude way; his eyes are unsteady and fickle; I am afraid of him."

Kiun made a sign of assent. But when they had arrived on the quay, Wang The-king gave himself so much trouble to find a junk and help to embark the luggage that the prefect, bound by the rites, could not avoid asking him to get on board the boat with him.

They unmoored; Wang The-king established himself on the prow with his wife, near the mariners; he spoke a long time with them while they were passing the last houses of the large city.

When night fell, they were in a part of the river where it got broader to such an extent that you could no longer distinguish the banks. The wind was blowing rather violently and the unfurling waves projected heavy showers on the mats which covered the quarter-deck.

Kiun, uneasy, went to the prow of the boat in order to question the master. The bright moon was rising, lighting the dark line of the bank. They approached in order to throw the anchor.

Wang The-king was on the narrow bridge; when Kiun came to his side, he coolly pushed the poor prefect overboard. Kiun's father was two paces behind; Wang ran to him and threw him also into the tumultuous waters of the rapid current. Kiun's mother, hearing a cry and a struggle, went to see what was happening, and she also was precipitated into the foaming river.

Seaweed, from the cabin, had seen all; but she took good care not to go outside; she moaned:

"Alas! my father-in-law and my mother-in-law are dead! My husband has been killed! I am going to die, too!"

While she was crying, Wang The-king entered the cabin.

"Fear nothing," said he; "forget those people who are no more and won't come back. I am going to take you home to the city of The-Golden-tombs. There I have fields and houses belonging to me; I will give them to you."

The young woman kept back her sobs and said nothing; she thought it wise not to provoke the murderer.

Wang The-king, very satisfied with his prospects, went back to the mariners, gave them the greater part of what his victims had brought in silver and luggage; then he quietly took his dinner and retired to his cabin with his wife. The woman had a strange look, but she did not say anything, and they went to sleep.

Towards the hour of the Rat, the woman began to groan; then she started out of her sleep and cried to her husband:

"Kill me, repudiate me! I can no longer stay with you! Thunder and lightning will strike you! I have dreamt it; I will no longer be the wife of a murderer and a thief!"

Wang, furious, struck her. But as she continued, he took her in his arms and threw her into the river.

On the second day the boat arrived at The-Golden-tombs. Wang took Seaweed to his family. When his old mother asked what he had done with his first wife, he replied:

"She fell in the river, and I will marry this one."

They were soon settled in the house. Wang wished to take liberties with Seaweed, who gently drove him back.

"We must not neglect the rites. Do not let us forget to empty first the marriage cup."

Wang joyously accepted; and soon, seated opposite each other, they began exchanging cups of wine in the ritual way.

Seaweed, however, pretended to drink, and tried to make her lover tipsy; she contrived this little by little.

Wang, rendered sleepy by the wine, undressed himself, got on the bed, and ordered the young woman to put out the lamps and come to him.

She carefully blew the lamps and said:

"I will come in a minute!"

Then she quickly went to her luggage, took out a sword she had hidden there, and came back. Feeling with her hands in the darkness, she found the throat of the man and struck him as hard as she could: the man screamed and tried to get up; she struck again and again: there was a moaning, a gurgle, and then silence.

However, Wang's mother, having heard some noise, came with a lantern. Seaweed killed her before the old woman could even say a word.

Then the young woman, having avenged her family, tried to cut her own throat, in order to join her husband. The sword was blunt and she was only able to scratch herself. She then remembered that, outside the house, there was a fairly big pond; she ran out and threw herself into the water.

Some neighbours saw her and ran to her help; other people came; lanterns were brought forth; the poor girl at last was taken out of the pond, and brought back to her house. But, when the new-comers entered the room, they saw the bodies and the blood.

"Murder! Murder!" cried they.

And they immediately sent a boy to call the police. The constables came and looked all over the room; they soon found in Seaweed's luggage a note prepared by the unfortunate woman and stating the truth about her family's death. The assistants were loud in their praise of her act:

"She avenged her husband; she has been witty enough to beguile the murderer; and now she has killed herself! Such an act of courage and virtue has not been heard of for centuries. We must ask the authorities to build her a marble arch to commemorate her history, and be an example to future generations."

While all this was going on, they tried to revive the woman; everything was done, but in vain. A coffin was then brought in, and the girl transferred to it, covered with her best garments and jewels. The lid was screwed on, and everybody left the house.

We must now come back to the evening when Wang pushed into the water Seaweed's husband. Kiun was a strong man and a very good swimmer; surprised by this sudden attack, all he could do at first was to keep his head out of the tumultuous water. He then thought to go back to the boat, but, on the foaming expanse nothing was to be seen; the rapid current had driven him too far. At last the water brought him to a curving beach, where he was able to land.

Walking disconsolately on the sand, he saw a human body rolled by the surge; he approached, and recognised his father; farther on he saw his mother; both he dragged out of the water. Most uneasy about his wife, he walked on the river's edge, straining his eyes; the moon was shining; he saw at last a human being holding a big piece of wood. He swam to her, pushed her to the beach, and took her he thought was his wife to the dry sand. He undid the upper garment in order to rub her members; when he saw she was not so cold, he wiped her hair out of her face. His stupor was immense in recognising Wang's wife.

The sun rose at last and warmed them. The young woman sighed, opened her eyes, and, completely herself again, told Kiun what she had seen:

"My husband is a murderer. In a dream I saw the King-of-Shadows himself sitting behind his tribunal and writing his name on the death-list. Besides, he is in love with your wife. If you wish it, we will go together straight to The Golden-tombs and do what we can to avenge ourselves."

Kiun, seeing a man coming to work in a field not far from there, went to him and told him in a few words what had happened; the man led them to his landlord, a rich man, who gave them food and warm dresses, sent men to bring the drowned bodies to a side house and have them properly buried. Then he advanced a certain sum of money to Kiun, who agreed to send it back when he should get to a place where he could find a correspondent of his bankers.

Then Kiun and his companion engaged a small boat and went down the river. When they got to The Golden-tombs, they questioned the people in the street about Wang. A month had elapsed since the events we have told of; the first man they questioned looked at them in wonder:

"How is it you don't know what happened? Wang is dead; he has been killed by a virtuous woman whose family he had murdered and who killed herself afterwards. You have only to go on; in the first street to your right you will see a new marble arch which has just been erected to commemorate virtuous Seaweed's courageous death."

Kiun thought his heart would burst; he dragged his companion to the marble arch and read the inscription. Then he bought a bundle of those imitations of gold and silver ingots made with paper which people burn on the tombs in order to send some money to the dead; he went to the tomb in the place indicated by the inscription.

There he reverently knelt, and, after having knocked the ground with his forehead, he burnt the paper-ingots, rose, and went away with Wang's wife.

When they were back in their boat, they discussed their plans and resolved to go down the river to Shanghai.

They were leaving the harbour, when a small boat crossed their way; two women sat on the bench. One of them reminded Kiun strangely of his late wife. The woman had looked up at him and seemed surprised. The retired prefect, moved by a mysterious strength, pronounced aloud a sentence which used to make his wife laugh when they were together happy in Hankow:

"I see wild geese flying high in the sky."

Seaweed, when she was alive, used to answer by a phrase which had nothing to do with the first sentence, and had made them laugh very often by its stupidity. The woman in the boat said it too:

"The dog wants the cat's biscuit; you quickly shut it in the house."

Kiun, wondering whether it was Seaweed's ghost, asked the mariners to go alongside the other boat; he jumped in it; the woman threw her arms round his neck, and they wept together.

"Are you alive? or is it only your ghost I hold in my arms?" asked he.

"I am alive!"

Then she told him her adventures; when she was put into the coffin, she had some jewels on. One of the assistants resolved to steal them; he waited till everybody was gone and the house empty; then he deliberately unscrewed the coffin's lid and rifled what he could. He was trying to take a ring off her hand, when the supposed corpse rose and screamed.

The poor man thought his last hour had come and did not move. Seaweed, seeing her jewels in his hands, and seeing the coffin she was in, grasped the situation at a glance.

"You want my jewels! Have them if you like; you saved my life, and without you I would have been stifled in this gruesome box."

The man at first dared not accept; then he said:

"In exchange for your kindness, I will tell you something. In the third house in the first street lives a rich widow; she is alone and would like to adopt a girl; go to her and tell her everything. She will be happy to give you a home."

Then he helped her to get out of the coffin, screwed the lid again, and disappeared. Seaweed went straight to the house. The widow received her with the greatest kindness, and asked of her to let everybody believe she was dead; if not, there would have been a lawsuit.

Both women, now united by the closest affection, had been out on the river for pleasure's sake when they saw Kiun's bark. The widow, when the explanations were finished, opened her arms to Kiun; she called him her son-in-law. Seaweed asked Wang's wife to be the second wife of her husband. And they all lived long and happy.

THE DUTIFUL SON

At the foot of the Oriental-Perfume-Mountain, in one of the most beautiful places of this celebrated district, the passers-by could see a small lodge. Chou The-favourable lived there with his mother. He was still young, being only thirty years old, and earned his living in the way so highly praised by the ancient Classics; he cultivated a small field by his house, and every week went to the next market to exchange what he had for what he wanted.

Both were very happy, when a calamity befell them; the old mother one morning felt a pain in her right leg. Two or three days afterwards she had there an ulcer that no remedies could cure; everything was tried and everything failed. Day and night she was moaning, turning over in her hard wooden bed.

The-favourable forgot to drink and eat, in his anxiety to give his mother the medicines the doctor advised.

Several months wore on; the ulcer did not heal. The despair of the son was greater every day; at last, overcome by his fatigue, he fell asleep and dreamt that he saw his father. The old man told him:

"You have been a dutiful son. But I must tell you that your mother will not recover if you can't apply to her ulcer a piece of man's fat."

Then everything was dissolved like a smoke in the wind.

The-favourable awoke and, thinking over his dream, he found it very strange.

"What can I do?" thought he. "Man's fat is not easily found in the market. My father would not have appeared to me if this extraordinary medicine was not really the only thing that will cure my mother. Well, I will take a piece of fat of my own body; I have nothing else to do."

Then, rising from his bed, he took a sharp knife, and, pulling the skin of his side, he cut a large piece off. His pain was not so great as he had expected it to be, and, what seemed more extraordinary to him, no blood flowed from the wound.

He could not see that, from the heaven above, a messenger had come on a cloud, was recording this noble feat on his life's register, and helped him by averting all ordinary sufferance.

The-favourable hastened to put the piece of flesh on his mother's ulcer; the pain disappeared immediately, and a few days after the old woman could walk as she used to do; on her leg there remained only a red scar.

When she asked what medicine had been employed, The-favourable eluded the answer. But somehow the truth was known in the neighbourhood; the prefect sent a report to the Throne and came himself with a decree of the Emperor, giving a title and an allowance to the dutiful son.

THROUGH MANY LIVES

Some people remember every incident of their former existences; it is a fact which many examples can prove. Other people do not forget what they learned before they died and were born again, but remember only confusedly what they were in a precedent life.

Wang The-acceptable, of the Yellow-peach-blossom city, when people discussed such questions before him, used to narrate the experience he had had with his first son.

The boy, at the time he spoke of, was three or four years old. He did not say many words, and some people thought he was dumb. One day, The-acceptable was writing a letter, when he was disturbed by a friend. He put his writing-brush down on the table and left the room. When he came back, his letter was finished, and written much more correctly than he would have believed himself able to do. Besides, he did not remember having finished it. The puzzle did not trouble him very much.

Another day the same thing occurred; he left the room, leaving a letter unfinished on the table; when he came back, the letter was nearly ended. Nobody but the boy had been in the room. Troubled and suspicious, he rose and feigned to go away; but he came back immediately and noiselessly. From the door, he saw his boy kneeling on the stool and writing the letter.

The little man suddenly saw his father and asked to be forgiven. The father of course laughed:

"We all thought you were dumb; if you are such a learned man, the family happiness will be great! How could we punish you?"

From that date he had good lessons given to the boy, who very early passed successfully his third degree examination and became one of the most celebrated "Entered among the learned" of his time.

When his father asked him whether he remembered what he had been before being what he now was, the boy said that the first life he could remember was that of a young student; he lived in a monastery to save as much as he could of his income. When he died, the King-of-the-Darkness punished him for his stinginess and condemned him to become a donkey in the same monastery he had lived in.

He wanted to die, but did not know what to do; the priests loved him and were very careful. One day he was on a mountain road and was tempted to throw himself downhill; but he had a man on his back and was afraid of the punishment the King-of-the-Darkness would inflict upon him if he killed that man. So he went on. Many years passed; he died at last, and was born again as a peasant. But, as he had forgotten nothing of his former lives, he was able to speak a few days after his birth. His father and mother judged the thing highly suspicious and killed him.

After that, he was born in the family of Wang The-acceptable. Appreciating the surroundings, and bearing in mind that he had last been killed because he spoke too early, he was very careful this time not to utter a single word. But when he saw the paper and ink he could not resist his love of literature and finished the letter.

THE RIVER OF SORROWS

Along the path leading to the city of All-virtues, in the obscure night, a poor coolie, grumbling under a heavy load of salt, was trudging on as fast as he could.

"I shall never get there before the hour of the Rat, and my wife will say again; 'Wang The-tenth has drunk too many cups of wine.' She does not know the weight of that stuff!"

As he was thus thinking, two men suddenly jumped from either side of the road and held him by the arms.

"What do you want?" cried the poor man. "I am only an unhappy carrier, and my load is only salt, very common salt."

"We don't want your salt, and you had better throw it down. We are sent from the Regions below and we want you to come down with us."

"Am I dead already?" asked The-tenth. "I did not know. I must tell my wife. Can't you come again to-morrow night?"

"Impossible to wait. You must come immediately. But I don't think you are dead. It is only to work for a few days down below."

"This is rather strange," replied The-tenth. "With all the people who have died since the world has been the world you still want living men? We don't go and ask you to do our work, do we?"

While thus arguing, he felt himself suffocated by a heavy smell and lost consciousness.

When he awoke, he was on the bank of a fairly large river. Hundreds of men were standing in the water; some of them carried baskets; others, with spades and different utensils, were dragging out what they could from the bottom. Soldiers with heavy sticks struck those who stopped even for a second.

On the bank several men were standing, and a number of others came from time to time. A magistrate was sitting behind a big red table, turning over the pages of a book. At last, he called "Wang The-tenth."

"Wang The-tenth!" repeated the soldiers. And they threw the poor man down in a kneeling position in front of the magistrate, who looked on the book and said:

"You have been an undutiful son; do you remember the day when you told your father he was a fool?"

Then speaking to the soldiers, he said:

"To the river!"

The guards pushed the man, gave him a basket, and ordered him to help in the cleaning of the river.

The water was red and thick; its stench was abominable; the bodies of the workmen were all red, and The-tenth discovered it was blood. He looked at the first basket he took to the bank; it was only putrid flesh and broken bones.

Thus he worked day by day without stopping. When he was not going fast enough, the guards struck him with their sticks, and their sticks were bones. In the deep places he had to put his head into the water and felt the filthy stuff fill his nostrils and mouth.

Among the workers he recognised many people he used to know. A great number died and were carried away by the stream.

At last two guards called his name, helped him to the bank, and suddenly he found himself again on the path leading to the city of All-virtues.

Now, on the night when The-tenth was taken away, his wife waited for him. Troubled not to see him, she started as soon as the sun beamed, and looked for him on the road. She soon found his body lying unconscious. Trying in vain to revive him, she thought him dead, and wept bitterly.

Not being strong enough to bring home his body, she came back to town in order to ask the help of her family. In the afternoon, clad in the white dress of mourning, and accompanied by her four brothers, she started again.

What was her astonishment and fear when, approaching the place where she had found the body, she saw her husband walking towards her. He was all covered with blood, and the stench was so strong that everybody pinched his nose.

When he had explained what had happened, they all returned to the village. The-tenth knelt reverently before his ancestors' tablet, offered butter and rice, and burnt incense.

This very day he asked a Taoist priest what was the river he had worked in. The priest explained to him it was called the River-of-sorrows. It took its source in the outer world in every tear that was shed. The people that killed themselves out of despair were floated down its stream to the kingdom of shadows.

Sometimes the sorrows on earth were so great that people killed themselves by thousands and did not shed any tears; the blood then was too thick to wash away the decayed remains, and the river-bed had to be cleaned lest it should overflow and drown the whole world. Living men alone were employed in this work, for only living men can cure living men's sorrows.

THE MYSTERIOUS ISLAND

In the beautiful Chu-san archipelago there is a small island where the flowers never cease blooming, and where the trees grow thick and high. From the most remote antiquity nobody has been known to live in the shade of this virgin forest; the ferns, the creepers, are so entangled that it is impossible for a man to cross this wilderness without clearing his way with a hatchet.

A young student named Chang, who lived in the City-over-the-sea, used to rest himself from his daily labour by going out to sea in a small junk he managed himself.

Having heard of the mysterious island, he resolved to explore it, prepared wine and food, and sailed out on a beautiful summer's morning.

Towards midday he neared the place where the island was supposed to be. Soon a delicious perfume of flowers was brought to him by the hot breeze. He saw the dark green of the trees over the light green of the sea, and, when still nearer, the yellow sand of the beach, where he resolved to disembark.

The junk touched the shore; he tied it to a large fallen tree whose end dipped into the gentle waves, and proceeded at once to a hearty meal.

While he was storing again in the boat what remained of his provisions, he was suddenly startled by a subdued laugh. Turning his head, he saw among the wild roses of the shore, a young girl covered with a long blue dress, who looked at him with dark eyes full of flame.

"Your servant is most happy to see you here. I did not suppose I should ever have the pleasure of meeting you."

"Who are you?" asked Chang, forgetting, in his astonishment, the proper forms of inquiry.

"I am only a poor singer who has been brought here by The-Duke-of-the-sea."

Chang, hearing these words, was afraid in his heart; The-Duke-of-the-sea was a renowned pirate who used to plunder every village of the coast, and was reputed to be cruel and vindictive. But the girl was so attractive that he soon forgot everything in the pleasure of her chatter.

Seated at the foot of a big tree, they were laughing, when a noise came from the forest.

"It is The-Duke-of-the-sea! It is The-Duke-of-the-sea!" murmured the girl. "I must be off at once."

And she disappeared behind the foliage.

While Chang was asking himself what he should do, he suddenly saw a huge snake coming straight to him. Its body was as thick as a cask, and so long that the end was still hidden in the forest, while the head was balancing over the frightened student.

Chang could not say a word and dared not move: the snake entwined himself round a tree and round the man, holding fast its prisoner's arms. Then, lowering its head, it threw out its tongue, and, pricking the student's nose, began to suck the blood which came out and fell on the ground.

Chang saw that, if he did not immediately free himself, he would certainly die. Feeling cautiously with his hand round his waist, he took from his purse a certain poisoned pill that he kept there and intended to try on wolves and foxes. With two fingers he took the pill and threw it into the red pool at his feet.

The snake, of course, sucked it with the blood; it immediately stopped drinking, straightened its body, and rocked its head to and fro, knocking the tree-trunks and hissing desperately.

Chang, feeble and hardly able to stand, dragged himself as fast as he could out of reach on to the beach and quickly untied his boat. Nevertheless, before going out to sea, he fetched a sword and went cautiously into the wood again. The snake did not move. Chang flourished his sword, and with a mighty stroke cut the head off and ran to his boat.

He returned to the City-over-the-sea, went to bed and was ill for a month. When he spoke of his experience, he always said that, to his mind, it was the beautiful girl he had seen at first who had come again in the form of a snake.

THE SPIRIT OF THE RIVER

In a small village along the river Tsz lived a fisherman named Siu. He started every night with his nets, and took very great care not to forget to bring with him a small jar of spirits. Before throwing his cast-net, he drank a small cup of the fragrant liquor and poured some drops into the slow current, praying aloud:

"O Spirit-of-the-river, please accept these offerings and favour your humble servant. I am poor and I must take some of the fishes that live in your cold kingdom. Don't be angry against me and don't prevent the eels and trouts coming to me!"

When every fisherman on the river brought back only one basket of fishes, he always proudly bore home a heavy charge of two or three baskets full to the brim.

Once, on a rosy dawn of early spring, when the sun, still below the horizon, began to eat with its golden teeth the vanishing darkness, he said aloud:

"O Spirit-of-the-river! For many years, every night I have drunk with you a good number of wine-cups; but I never saw your face; won't you favour me with your presence? We could sit together, and the pleasure of drinking would be much greater."

Hardly had he finished these words when, from the middle of the stream, emerged a beautiful young man clothed in pink, who slowly walked on the smooth surface of the limpid water, and sat on the boat's end, saying:

"Here I am."

The fisherman, being half-drunk, was not troubled in any way; he bowed to the young man, offered him, with his two hands, a cup of the strong wine, and said:

"Well! I long wished to receive your instructions, and I am very glad to see you. You must be mighty tired of living in that water; the few drops of wine I pour every night are quite lost in such a quantity of tasteless liquid. You had better come up every night; we will drink together and enjoy each other's company."

From this day, when darkness closed in, the Spirit waited for the fisherman and partook of his provisions. As soon as the sun rose above the horizon he suddenly disappeared. The fisherman did not find that very convenient; he asked his companion if he could not arrange to stay with him sometimes in the daytime.

"Impossible; we can't do such a thing, we spirits and ghosts. We belong to the kingdom of shadows. When the shadows, fighting the daylight, bring with them the Night, we are free to go and wander about. But as soon as the herald of the morn, the cock, has proclaimed the daily victory of the sun, we are powerless and must disappear."

On the same day the fisherman was sitting on the bank, smoking a pipe before going home with his baskets, when he saw a woman holding a child in her arms and hastening along the river towards a ford some hundred yards up stream. She was already in the water, when she missed her footing, fell into the river, and was rolled away by the stream. The child, by some happy chance, had fallen on the bank and lay there, crying.

The fisherman could easily have gone in his boat and saved the woman, who was still struggling to regain the bank, but he was a prudent man:

"This woman, whom I don't know, seems to be beautiful," thought he. "Maybe it is my friend The-Spirit-of-the-river who has arranged all this, and chosen the girl to be his wife. If I prevent her going down to his cold lodgings, he will be angry and ruin my fishing. All I could do is to adopt this boy until somebody comes and asks for him."

And he did not move, until the poor woman had disappeared in the yellow stream; then he took the child. Once back in the village, he inquired about the mother; nobody could tell who she was. The days passed and nobody asked for the boy. This was strange enough, but, stranger still, from this day the fisherman never saw The-Spirit-of-the-river again. He offered him many cups of wine, and his fishing was as good as ever, but though he prayed heartily, his companion of so many nights did not appear any more.

When the boy was three years old he insisted on accompanying his adopted father in his night fishing. Summer had come; the cold was no more to be feared. The man consented to take his adopted son with him; they started together in the twilight.

As soon as the darkness closed, the boy's voice changed; his appearance was different.

"What a silly man you are!" said he. "Don't you know me now? For more than two years I waited for an opportunity to tell you who I was. But you always went out at night and you never came back before the sun was high in the sky. You had never failed to present your offerings; so I could not resist your prayer when you asked me to stay with you in the daytime. Now, here I am, till your death; when the sun is up I shall only be your son, but when the night closes I shall be your companion, and we will enjoy together what longevity the Fate allows you."

THE-DEVILS-OF-THE-OCEAN

In the twenty-second year of the period Eternal-happiness, the population of Chao-cheou's harbour, awaking on a bright summer's morning, were extremely surprised and frightened to see, swaying on the blue water of the bay, a strange and abnormally huge ship. The three high masts were heavily loaded with transversal pieces of wood, from some of which sails were still hanging; another mast projected horizontally from the prow, and three sails were tightened from this to the foremast.

A small boat was lowered from the ship's side and rowed to the quay. Several hundreds of people were watching the proceedings, asking one another if it was a human invention or a ship coming from the depths of hell.

The small boat stopped at a short distance from the bank; one could see that, beside the rowers, there were three men seated in the stern; their heads were covered with extraordinarily long and fluffy grey hair; they wore big hats with feathers of many colours. A Chinaman was in the boat and hailed the people:

"Ha! Please tell the local authorities that high mandarins from the ocean want to speak to them. We are peaceful. But if you do any harm to our men or ships, our wrath will be such that we will destroy in one day the whole town and kill everybody within ten miles' distance."

Three or four men belonging to the Yamen had heard these words; they ran to the prefect's palace and came back with an answer they delivered to the new-comers:

"His Excellency the prefect consents to receive your visit. If you are peaceful, no harm will be done to you. But if you steal anything, or wound or kill anybody, the laws of our country will be enforced upon you without mercy."

Then the boat slowly accosted the quay; two of the men with feathered hats disembarked with the Chinaman, while six of the rowers, leaving their oars in the boat, shouldered heavy muskets, and cleared the way, three walking in front of the feathered hats and three behind. The rowers wore small caps and had long blue trousers and very short blue coats.

The prefect, in his embroidered dress, awaited them on the threshold of his reception-room. He bade the new-comers be seated and asked their names and their business; the Chinaman translated the questions and the answers.

"We come from the other side of the earth."

"Well," thought the prefect. "I was sure of it, the earth being square and flat, the other side of it is certainly hell. What am I to do?"

"We only want to trade with your countrymen. We will sell you what goods we have brought; we will buy your country's productions, and if no harm is done we will sail away in a few days."

"Our humble country is very poor," answered the prefect. "The people are not rich enough to buy any of the splendid goods you may have brought. Besides, this country's products are not worth your giving any money for them. If I can give you good advice, you had better sail away to-day and get to the first harbour of the northern province; there they are very rich."

"We have just come from it; they told us the very reverse. Here, according to them, we should be able to find everything we want. Besides, our mind is settled; we will remain here long enough to buy what we want and to sell what we can. We are very peaceful people as long as one deals justly with us. But if you try to beguile us, we will employ all our strength in the defence of our rights. All we want is a place on shore where we can store and show our goods."

"Well, well; I never intended to do anything of the sort," said the prefect. "But the Emperor is the only possessor of the soil. How could I give you a place even on the shore?"

"We don't want very much, and the Emperor won't know anything. Give us only the surface of ground covered by a carpet, and we will be satisfied."

Chinese carpets are not more than two or three feet broad and five or six feet wide. The prefect thought he could not be blamed to authorise the foreigners to settle on such a small piece of ground; on the other hand, if he refused, there would ensue trouble and he would certainly be cashiered.

"It is only as a special arrangement and by greatly compromising with the law that I can give you this authorisation."

And the prefect wrote a few words on one of his big red visiting-cards. The interpreter carefully perused the document. Then the foreigners went back to their ship. The same day a proclamation was issued and pasted on the walls of the public edifices, explaining to the people that The-Devils-of-the-ocean had been authorised to settle on a piece of ground not bigger than a carpet and that no harm should be done to them.

In compliance with these orders, nobody dared oppose the foreigners when they began unrolling on the shore a carpet ten yards broad and thirty yards long. When the carpet was unrolled, The-Devils-of-the-ocean put themselves in ranks with muskets and swords on the carpet; nearly five hundred men stood there close to one another.

The prefect, who had personally watched the proceeding, was so angry against the foreigners for their cunningness that he immediately ordered troops to drive them out into the water. But the foreigners had a devilish energy nobody could resist; they killed a great many of our people, burned the greater part of the city, and occupied for several years all the northern part of the bay, where they erected a sort of bazaar and a fortress, which still exist to this day.

UNKNOWN DEVILS

Suen Pure-whiteness was privileged with the possibility of seeing distinctly all the creatures of the other world, who, for the greater part of humanity, remain always mysterious and invisible.

One night he slept in a mountain monastery; he had closed and barred the door; the full moon illuminated the window; everything was quiet. He had slept an hour, when he was awakened by the hissing of the wind; the gate of the monastery seemed to be thrown open; after a while the door of his room was shaken, the bar dropped down, and the heavy wood turned on its hinges.

Pure-whiteness thought at first that it would be better to close his eyes and to wait; but his curiosity was aroused, he looked intently; after a few seconds he could see a big devil, so big that he was obliged to stoop in order not to break his head against the ceiling, and who was coming slowly towards the bed. His face had the colour and general appearance of an old melon. His eyes were full of lightning and his mouth was bigger than a tub. His teeth were at least three inches long and his tongue kept moving incessantly, while he uttered a sound like "Ha-la."

Pure-whiteness was much afraid; but, seeing he had no way of escape, he took a short sword from under his pillow and, with all his might, thrust it into the devil's breast; it sounded as if he had struck a stone.

The devil hissed in a fearful way; he extended his claws to catch the man. Pure-whiteness jumped on the right side; the devil could only catch his dress and started; the man hastened to unfasten his dress; he dropped and remained there on all fours, motionless and mute. When the devil's steps ceased to be heard he screamed for help; the priests came with lamps; everything was in order, but in the bed Pure-witeness was yelling as in a nightmare.

On another day Pure-whiteness was in the country enjoying the pleasures of harvest. The golden rice was piled high and everybody was busy. Some armed men had been posted here and there, according to the custom; everybody knows that when the rice is ripened in a place, people of the neighbouring villages are always looking for an opportunity to make the harvest themselves or to take away what has been cut by the owners.

Pure-whiteness, tired by the heat, laid down behind a rice-stack; after a while he heard stealthy steps; raising his head, he saw a big devil more than ten feet high, with hair and beard of a fierce reddish colour, who was approaching. Pure-whiteness yelled for help: men with spears came to the rescue. The devil bellowed like the thunder and flew away. Pure-whiteness told them what he had seen; nobody would believe him, but they nevertheless started in pursuit; people working in the fields all round had not seen anything, so everybody came back.

The second day Pure-whiteness was among four or five men, when he saw the same devil.

"He has come back!" cried he, flying away.

The other people ran away too. When they came back, everything was quiet. But they always kept by their side some spears, bows and arrows, and swords.

For two or three days, they had no trouble; the rice was being stored in the granaries, when Pure-whiteness, looking up, screamed:

"The devil has come back!"

Everybody ran to his arms. Pure-whiteness fell down; the devil picked him up, bit his head, threw him down, and went away.

When the man came back, Pure-whiteness bore the marks of teeth on his head; he did not know anybody. Taken home and nursed, he remained unconscious for a few days and died.

CHILDLESS

In the city of The-Great-name lived a rich idler named Tuan Correct-happiness. He had then attained the age of forty and still he had no son. His wife, Peaceful-union, was extremely jealous, so that he dared not openly buy a concubine, as law authorised him, to continue his lineage.

When he saw that, at forty, he had no son, he secretly bought a young girl, whom he carefully left outside his own house.

A woman is not easily deceived—a jealous woman especially; Peaceful-union soon discovered the whole truth. She had the girl brought before her and took advantage of an impertinent answer to have her beaten a hundred blows; after that, she turned on her husband and drove him nearly mad with reproaches. What could the poor man do? He sold his concubine to a neighbouring family named Liu, and peace was restored in the house.

The days and years passed on without any change in the situation; the nephews of Correct-happiness, seeing that he was old already and had no son, began to fawn upon him, each of them trying to be the one that would be elected as an adopted son to continue the family cult, as is the custom.

Peaceful-union at last began to see her error and regretted bitterly what she had done.

"You are only sixty years old," said she to her husband. "Is it too late? Let us buy two chosen girls who will be your second wives; maybe one of them will give you a son."

The old man smiled sadly; he did not entertain any great hope; nevertheless, the concubines were bought. After a year, to the great surprise and joy of everybody, both gave birth—one to a girl, the other to a boy. But both children died a few months after.

Correct-happiness, when winter set in, caught a cold and was soon in a desperate state of health. His nephews were always beside him; but, seeing he would adopt neither of them, they began looting the house; they found at last the treasure and took it away openly.

The moribund was too ill even to know what they did. Peaceful-union tried in vain to stop them.

"Will you leave me to die of hunger? I am the wife of your uncle. I am entitled to a part of his riches."

But they would not hear her.

"If you had borne a son to our uncle, or if he had adopted one of us, we would not have touched a single copper cash of his treasure; but, through your own fault, he has nobody to maintain his rights; we take what is our own."

When the day ended, the widow found herself alone in the deserted and emptied house, crying over the body of her dead husband.

Suddenly she heard steps outside the door; a young man appeared on the threshold, his eyes full of tears, covered with the white dress of mourning. He entered, kneeled beside the corpse, and, knocking the ground with his forehead, he began the ritual lamentations.

Peaceful-union stopped crying and looked at him with astonishment; she did not know him.

"May I ask your noble name? Who are you to cry over my husband's death?"

"I am the deceased's only son."

The widow started with surprise and a pang of her old jealousy; would her husband have had a son without her knowing it? But the next words of the young man explained everything.

Twenty years ago, when she had beaten and sold away the first concubine of her husband, she did not know the girl bore already the fruit of this short union. Six months later she had a son, to whom she gave the name of Correct-sadness; but, bearing in mind the bad treatment she had received, she asked the Liu family to keep the child as one of their own. They consented and sent the boy to school with their children.

When Correct-sadness was eighteen, the chief of the Liu family died; the family dispersed, and only a small legacy was left to the young man. Believing he was a member of the family, he could not understand what happened, and asked his mother; she told him the truth. Resenting the hard treatment inflicted on his mother, he awaited the death of his father to make his own identity known.

Peaceful-union was very happy to hear this story.

"I am no more without a son," said she. "All that my nephews have taken away, treasure and furniture, they must bring back again. If not, the magistrate will send them to die in jail."

In fact, the nephews refused to give back anything. The widow began a lawsuit; everything at last was restored to the legal heir.

Peaceful-union hastened to choose him a wife, and as soon as the matrimonial festivities were ended she told her daughter-in-law:

"My dear child, if I were you, I would ask Correct-sadness to buy immediately one or two good concubines; if you have a son and they have also, so much the better, but you can't realise how difficult to bear it is to be childless."

THE PATCH OF LAMB'S SKIN

In the twenty-fourth year K'ang-hsi lived in a remote district of the western provinces, a man who could remember his former lives. He was now a "tsin-shi," "entered-among-the-learned," renowned, and much considered by his friends.

When speaking of the existences he had gone through, he used to say:

"As far as I remember, I was first a soldier—it was in the last days of the Ming dynasty; my regiment was encamped at The-Divided-roads on the Ten-thousand-miles-great-wall. My remembrances are not very clear as to whom we fought with, but I remember the joy of striking the enemy, the hissing of the arrows, the yelling of the charging troops.

"I was still young when I was killed. After death, of course I was called before the tribunal of The-King-of-shadows. Closing my eyes, I can still see the big caldrons full of boiling oil for the trying of criminals; the Judge in embroidered dress seated behind a red table; the satellites everywhere, ready to act on the first word,—in fact, everything exactly the same as in the worldly tribunals, excepting that, in the eastern part of the hall, there were huge wooden stands from which hung skins of every description—horse-skins, lambs' skins, dogs' skins, and human skins of every age and condition; skins of old men, of fat and important people, of lean and shrivelled men, of boys and girls.

"The trial began; the souls, according to their deeds, were condemned to put on one of the skins and to come up again to the Lighted World in this new shape.

"When my turn came I was sentenced to put a dog's skin on; and in this low shape I was thrown again in the stream of life. But as I had not forgotten my former condition, I was so ashamed, that the first day I came on earth I threw myself under the wheels of a heavy carriage and died.

"The-King-of-shadows was extremely surprised to see me again so soon; the dogs, as a rule, having no conscience, he could not suppose I had killed myself, and did not hold me responsible for it.

"This time, I was born again as a pig. Pigs are valuable, and there are always people to look after them; so I could not kill myself. I tried to starve myself to death, but hunger was the strongest, and I had to endure such a life. Happily, the butcher soon put a speedy end to it.

"When my name was called to the tribunal of Darkness, the King-of-shadows looked over the pages of the Book and said:

"'He must be a lamb now.'

"The runners took a white lamb's skin, brought it, and began putting it over my body. While this was going on, the secretary, who was writing the sentence in the Book, started and said to the Judge:

"'Your Honour, there is a mistake. Please Your Honour read over again; this soul has to be a man now.'

"You know that, on the Big Book of Shadows, all our past deeds are recorded as well as our future destiny.

"The Judge looked at it over again and said:

"'True! Happily, you saw the mistake.'

"Then, turning to the runners, he ordered them to take off the skin, which already covered more than half my body. They had to exert all their strength, and even so, they tore it off into pieces. It hurt me so much that I thought I could not stand it and I should die; but I was dead, and I could not die more than that.

"At last they left me bleeding and panting, and I was born again in my present condition. But they had forgotten a piece of lamb's skin on my right shoulder, and I still have it now."

And he uncovered his arm and shoulder to show a piece of white woollen hair on his right shoulder.

LOVE'S-SLAVE

In the City-between-the-rivers lived a young student named Lan. He had just passed successfully his second literary examination, and, walking in the Street-of-the-precious-stones, asked himself what he would now do in life.

While he was going, looking vacantly at the passers-by, he saw an old friend of his father, and hastened to join his closed fists and to salute him very low, as politeness orders.

"My best congratulations!" answered the old man. "What are you doing in this busy street?"

"Nothing at all; I was asking myself what profession I am now to pursue."

"What profession? Which one would be more honourable than that of teacher? It is the only one an 'elevated man' *Kiu-jen* of the second degree, can pursue. By the by, would you honour my house with your presence? My son is nearly eighteen. He is not half as learned as he should be, and, besides, he has a very bad temper. I feel very old; if I knew you would consent to give him the right direction and be a second father to him, I would not dread so much to die and leave him alone."

Lan bowed and said:

"I am much honoured by your proposition, and I accept it readily. I will go to-morrow to your palace."

Two hours after, a messenger brought to the young man a packet containing one hundred ounces of silver, with a note stating that this comparatively great sum represented his first year's salary.

In the evening he knocked at his pupil's door and was ushered into the sitting-room. The old man introduced him to the whole family: first his son, a lad with a decided look boding no good; then a young and beautiful girl of seventeen, his daughter, called Love's-slave. Lan was struck by the sweet and refined appearance of his pupil's sister.

"The sight of her will greatly help me to stay here," thought he.

The next morning, when his first lesson was ended, he strolled out into the garden, admiring here a flower and there an artificial little waterfall among diminutive mountain-rocks. Behind a bamboo-bush he suddenly saw Love's-slave and was discreetly turning back, when she stopped him by a few words of greeting.

Every day they thus met in the solitude of the flowers and trees and grew to love each other. Lan's task with his pupil was greater and harder than he had supposed; but for Love's-slave's sake, he would never have remained in the house.

After three months the old man fell ill; the doctors were unable to cure him; he died, and was buried in the family ground, behind the house.

When Lan, after the funeral, told his pupil to resume his lessons, he met with such a reception that he went immediately to his room and packed his belongings. Love's-slave, hearing from a servant what had happened, went straight to her lover's room and tried to induce him to stay.

"How can you ask that from me?" said he. "After such an insult, I would consider myself as the basest of men if I stayed. I have 'lost face'; I must go."

The girl, seeing that nothing could prevail upon his resolution, went out of the room, but silently closed and locked the outer gate.

Lan left on a table what remained of the silver given him by the old man, and wrote a note to inform his pupil of his departure.

When he tried the gate and found it locked, he did not know at first what to do. Then he remembered a place where he could easily climb over the enclosure, went there, threw his luggage over the wall, and let himself out in this somewhat undignified way.

Before going back to his house, he went round to the tomb of the old man and burnt some sticks of perfume. Kneeling down, he explained respectfully to the dead what had happened and excused himself for having left unfinished the task he had undertaken. Rising at last, he went away.

The next morning Love's-slave, pleased with her little trick, came to the student's room and looked for him; he was nowhere to be found. She saw the silver on the table, and, reading the note he had left, she understood that he would never come back.

Her grief stifled her; heavy tears at last began running down her rosy cheeks. She took the silver, went straight to her father's tomb, fastened the heavy metal to her feet, and unrolled a sash from her waist. Then, making a knot with the sash round her neck, she climbed up the lower branches of a big fir-tree, fastened the other end of the coloured silk as high as she could and threw herself down. A few minutes afterwards she was dead. She was discovered by a member of the family, and quietly buried in the same enclosure.

Lan, who did not know anything, came back two or three days after to see her. The servants told him the truth. Silently and sullenly, he went to the tomb, and long remained absorbed in his thoughts; dusk was gathering; the first star shone in the sky. All of a sudden, hearing a sound as of somebody laughing, he turned round. Love's-slave was before his eyes.

"I was waiting for you, my love," she said in a strange and muffled voice. "Why are you coming so late?"

As he wanted to kiss her, she stopped him:

"Oh dear! I am dead. But it is decreed that I will come again to life if a magician performs the ceremony prescribed in the Book-of-Transmutations."

Immaterial like an evening fog, she disappeared in the growing darkness.

Lan returned immediately to the town, and, entering the first Taoist temple he saw, he explained to the priest what he wanted.

"If she has said it is decreed she should come back to life, we have only to go and open her tomb, while here my disciples will sing the proper chapters of the Book. Let us go now."

Giving some directions to his companions, he took a spade and started with Lan. The moon was shining, so that without any lantern they were able to perform their gloomy task.

Once the heavy lid of the coffin was unscrewed and taken off, the body of the young girl appeared as fresh as if she had been sleeping.

When the cold night-air bathed her face, she raised her head, sneezed, and sat up; looking at Lan, she said in a low voice:

"At last, you have come! I am recalled to life by your love. But now I am feeble; don't speak harshly to me; I could not bear it."

Lan, kissing her lovingly, took her in his arms and brought her to his house. After some days she was able to walk and live like ordinary people do.

They married and lived happily together for a year. Then, one day, Lan, having come back half-drunk from a friend's house, was rebuked by her, and, incensed, pushed her back. She did not say a word but, fainting, she fell down. Blood ran from her nostrils and mouth; nothing could recall her departing spirit.

THE LAUGHING GHOST

Siu Long-mountain was one of the most celebrated students of the district of Perfect-flowers. Having mastered the mysterious theories of the ancient Classics, he took a fancy in the researches of the Taoist magicians, whose temples may be found in the smallest villages of the Empire. He soon discovered that, for the greater number, they were impostors; and, being proud of his newly acquired science, he concluded that none of them possessed any occult power.

When he came to this somewhat hasty conclusion, he was seated alone in his library; the night was already advancing; a small oil lamp hardly illuminated his books on the table he was sitting at.

"Yes, there is no doubt; nothing exists outside the material appearances. There is nothing occult in the world, and nothing can come out of nothingness."

As he was saying these words half aloud, he was startled by an unearthly laugh which seemed to come from behind his back. He turned quickly round; but nothing was to be seen.

His heart beating, he was listening intently; the laugh came from another part of the room.

Long-mountain was brave, but as people are brave who have only met the ordinary dangers of civilised life, such as barking dogs, insulting coolies, or angry dealers presenting a long-deferred bill. He tried in vain to believe it was only a joke imposed on him by some friend; nothing could prevail upon his growing terror.

Straining his eyes, he looked at the part of the room the laugh seemed to come from. At first he could not see anything, but by degrees he perceived a black shadow moving in a corner, then a strange form with a horse's head and a man's body, all covered with long black hair; the teeth were big and sharp as so many mountain-peaks. The eyes of this dreadful creature began shining so much that the whole room was illuminated. Then it began moving towards the man.

This was too much; the student screamed like a dying donkey, and, bursting the door open, he ran out into the courtyard.

From an open door in the western pavilion a ray of light crossed the darkness; four or five men were playing cards, drinking, and swearing. Long-mountain ran into their room, and, panting, explained his vision.

The men, being drunk, wanted to see the Thing; holding lanterns and lamps, they accompanied their visitor back to his studio. When they passed the doorway, Long-mountain screamed again; the Thing was still there. He would have run away had not the men, laughing and jesting, shown him what the Ghost in reality was—a long dress hung in a corner to a big hook, on which sat a black cat mewing desperately.

When the men closed the door and left him alone, the student was deeply ashamed of his terror; shaken by his emotion, he went to bed and tried to sleep. Sleep would not come; his nervousness seemed to increase. Starting at the smallest noise, he remained a long time wide awake; then he lost consciousness.

In the silence one only heard the cries of the night-birds and the buzzing of the autumn's insects; the lamp was out, but a brilliant moon began to pour its silver light through the window.

The door suddenly creaked; Long-mountain awoke and sat up on his bed; the door slowly opened, and the same Thing he had seen and heard entered the room and advanced towards the bed, while the same unearthly laugh came from the long and unshapely head; the flaming eyes were fixed on the student.

When the Thing was near the bed, Long-mountain fell heavily and did not move any more.

The Ghost stopped, put his hand on the breast of the man, remained in that position a moment, then went quickly and silently out of the room.

A man was standing outside.

"What did he say?" asked he.

"Be quiet!" said the Ghost, taking off his horse's head and discovering a man's very serious face. "The joke was good. But we have done it too well. I think he is dead of terror; we had better be as silent as a tomb about all this. The magistrate would never believe in a joke; we would be held responsible for this death and pay a heavy penalty."

THE END

Milton Keynes UK
Ingram Content Group UK Ltd.
UKHW030913151124
451262UK00006B/783